# Sailing
### The
# Inland
# Seas

## Further Adventures
## Of Two
## Sunset Sailors

By
Paul H. Keller

Illustrated By Emily T. Keller

## Portside Publishing

Portland, Oregon

For information address:

Portside Publishing Company
9498 SW Barbur Blvd.  Suite 305
Portland, Oregon 97219

Text and Cover Design:
ICON Presentations
74 Wheatherstone Ct.
Lake Oswego, Oregon 97035

*DEDICATION:*

To Iris, Alex and Nicholas
This Grandfather's Heritage

## ACKNOWLEDGEMENTS

What makes a book? First, I suppose, you must have an author, and he or she must write it. Next, you need an illustrator and with great love and affection I acknowlege in that role my wife Emily. Next you need an editor to find your grammatical, spelling, and typo errors, and more important to suggest revisions in order and rhetoric. In that role I cast Sandra Dorr, the most efficient and helpful of any I have ever met and I don't ever expect to meet her superior. The layout and much of the cover art was produced by John E. Hanan II and associates of ICON Presentations.

The greatest joy of all was the encouragement and, yes, a push now and then from our friend and marketing director, Sharon Castlen of Nelsen and Associates. Sharon's boundless energy and knowledge of her profession was the principal reason that our first book succeeded.

Emily and I hope that these people have all joined into our life in such a way that this book will bring pleasure to others.

Paul H. Keller

March 20, 1994

Old age hath yet his honor and his toll;
Death closes all: but something ere the end,
Some work of noble note, may yet be done,
Not unbecoming men that strove with Gods.
The lights begin to twinkle from the rocks:
The long day wanes: the slow moon climbs:
The deep moans round with many voices.
Come my friends,
"Tis not too late to seek a newer world.
Push off, and sitting well in order smite
The sounding furrows; for my purpose holds
To sail beyond the sunset, and the baths
Of all the western stars, until I die.
It may be we shall touch the Happy Isles,
And see the great Achilles, whom we knew.
Tho' much is taken, such abides; and tho'
We are not now that strength which in old days
Moved earth and heaven; that which we are,
We are; one equal temper of heroic hearts,
Made weak by time and fate, but strong in will
To strive, to seek, to find, and not to yield.

*From Ulysses by Alfred Lord Tennyson*

# Sailing the Inland Seas

## TABLE OF CONTENTS

## PREFACE

This is the second book that chronicles the adventures of two Sunset Sailors, Emily and myself, who retired, fell in love, and sailed around the world. I was 64 years old when I sailed Golden Fleece, a 28 foot sailboat, down the Columbia River and out into the vast Pacific Ocean. We sailed the Pacific, the Mediteranean, part of the Atlantic, the Caribbean, the canals and rivers of France, and the great American heartland waterways. Come with us while we tour a bit of the Caribbean and the Eastern United States on a new boat that we grew to love. These canals and rivers which we sailed were traveled by our ancestors and were the principal way that commerce moved in those days. There is still commerce, but our view from the water was very bucolic. We will travel the same watery highways first traveled by Indians, then the trappers, then the settlers, all replaced now by huge tugs and barges, steamships, and pleasure boats like ours. Except for occasional towns and cities we were exposed to a feast of wildlife, vistas of raw wilderness and local characters that were delightfully charming.

Those who have read our first book, *Sailing the Golden Seas*, know that our books are also about a love affair that ripened in our senior years and the determination of one of us to fullfill a life-long dream, and the other who had the courage and love to go with him. They will also, we hope, encourage others who may have such dreams, and need a little boost to their courage to fullfill them.

As a teen-ager I was a copious reader, and since I grew up in a small town in Nebraska, the romance of far away places and the adventures of sailing had great appeal to me living as I did in a dusty Nebraska town. Through the years while I fullfilled my obligations as a family man I dabbled with the sea and sailing when, after graduating from college I moved to Portland, Oregon. As the nest emptied of children the gulf between myself and my wife widened and we went our separate ways. I dove into sailing with a zest and worked toward my goal. Sailing my own small boats, crewing for others, taking courses to improve my boating skills and living on board — all done to prepare me for my big adventure. I retired from my position as a college professor, purchased a world-class cruising boat and prepared it for the great adventure. Only one thing was lacking — someone with whom to share the dream.

Enter, Emily, the trim and adventurous lady of 59 years. Her tales of traveling to the Mt. Everest base camp in Nepal, skiing into Yellowstone in mid-winter, climbing mountains, and many other adventures certainly indicated the proper spirit. She was a doctor, teaching at the Oregon Health Sciences University, an artist and a good conversationalist. I learned all this while giving her a lesson in skiing while I was enjoying the status of weekend ski instructor the last year before I had determined to leave.

By cleverly manipulating one another, we became engaged just before I had planned to depart for the South Pacific. I left on the scheduled date. Half-way down the coast to Cabo San Lucas, Mexico, during a phone call we agreed not to put off the marriage any longer, so I flew home and we were married. I left her the day after we were married — to return to the boat knowing that she would join me in Tahiti the next July when she would be retired. Which she did, and our nine years of married life afloat have been a continual saga of adventure and happiness.

The point of this preface is that anyone in good health who wants to live his golden years fullfilling the dreams he has cherished, can do so. It takes only the courage to "strike out", prepare, then DO IT!

As Ulysses said in Tennyson's poem, "Come my friends, 'tis not too late to seek a newer world. Push off, and sitting well in order smite the sounding furrows."

Paul H. Keller

Portland, Oregon

## 1

# ACQUIRING ELIZABETH M

When we first saw Elizabeth M our hearts jumped. We were pretty discouraged. We'd been looking at boats and were down to the last one that would fit our requirements. She was a thirty eight foot motor sailor of a type we had seen before and liked but each one of this model had flaws that were major enough to cause us to reject them. But this beautiful creature seemed to have everything, including an aura of personality that exuded integrity and comfort. This was the boat that we would use touring the Eastern United States via its rivers, lakes and canals.

I have many friends who have retired and toured the

United States by motor home. But another way to tour a large part of the U. S. is by boat. Facing this page is a map of Eastern United States with all its navigable rivers, lakes, reservoirs and canals. You can see that a great pathway of watery highways criss crosses the eastern part of the country. When we discovered this remarkable system, Emily and I decided to buy a boat and spend a year or more exploring these watery highways, starting in Florida and returning there in a circumnavigation of the eastern U.S.

The idea reached a conclusive stage while we were still in Europe touring the Mediterranean. Golden Bell, our 32 foot ketch, was an excellent craft for crossing the Atlantic, but we wanted a different boat for cruising in the U. S. waters. When our Atlantic crossing was thwarted by a 10-day storm off the coast of Africa, we left our beloved Golden Bell in the hands of a yacht broker in Spain and flew to the East Coast of the U. S. to begin a search for a new floating home.

We drew up in our minds the specifications for our *ultimate* live-aboard home, and as we discussed them with yacht broker Barbara in Annapolis, Maryland, it became clear that we were describing a motor-sailor that we had seen frequently in the Mediterranean — the Nauticat, built in Finland. By computer Barbara located six Nauticats on the East Coast and checked out their availability. Only three were still on the market: one in Annapolis, one in Texas, and one in Puerto Rico. So, along with a look at a couple of other designs, we started our search. For the uninformed, a motor-sailor differs from a "sailboat" in two ways: it has a large engine, usually with about twice as much power as a normal sailboat of the same size, and it has inside steering. The helmsman is protected from the cold winds and spray

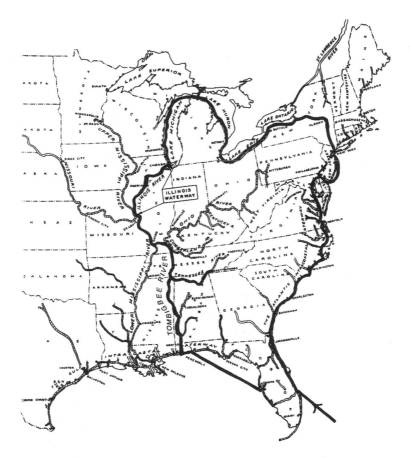

which are considered normal discomforts of sailing. To my mind, a chap of my advanced years has earned his comforts and has little need to prove his manhood or grit.

And we wanted more room in a boat, as do all live-aboard's who sail the world's seas. Emily, particularly, wanted to be able to spread out her brushes and paints without feeling guilty about taking up practically the whole boat. Now that we were back in the states, we also expected many more visits from friends and needed more space and privacy for them.

The Nauticat in Annapolis was too sterile. Another motor-sailor had poor layout and too little sail to move her in anything but a gale. Another sailboat that Barbara wanted us to see seemed to have less interior space than Golden Bell — which was six feet shorter!

Down we went to Fort Lauderdale to inspect two or three other boats. We lingered at Emily's request over a motor-sailor that had a washer and dryer on board but it resembled a Dutch barge boat with a short mast, and again would require a full gale to get her moving. Oh, well, we had survived the last six years doing our laundry in a bucket or in shore-side coin machines. After all, if this luxury were important we would never have gone cruising.

This left only the Nauticats in Texas and Puerto Rico. We bought tickets for Texas. Shortly before leaving, we got a frantic call from Barbara's colleague that the Texas boat had been sold. Before we could change our tickets to Puerto Rico, he called again to tell us that Barbara had spotted the Puerto Rico boat in Tortola, where she was vacationing and she would meet us there. We changed our tickets to Tortola without the slightest idea where the island was located. The ticket seller, apparently having no problem with its location, punched out the exchange. We learned later that the Nauticat's owner, despairing after a year that his boat would sell, had continued cruising. Barbara contacted us at our hotel shortly after we arrived and said that she would get us aboard at 10 a.m. the next morning. Tortola, by the way, is in the British Virgin Islands, and, one of the nicest islands we had visited since the South Pacific.

Emily and I were too excited to wait much longer but we did realize that we were going to visit somebody's home and not a bare boat. We, having lived aboard for almost six years and fully conversant with the fact that where one lives is not always the epitome of cleanliness and tidiness, readily assented to a delay of a few hours. The first mate, such as Emily, wants all the dishes clean and stowed, the beds neatly made and all the ports (windows) clean, the head (toilet) cleaned and fresh linen everywhere. The Captain wants all the lines coiled, the deck swabbed, the anchor stowed, and a full battery and the electronics all working. As, around any land-based home, neatness and orderliness are not always present and so we respected their request for a delay.

To explain things further, we who live aboard small boats and cruise the world do not see them as just a thing to amuse us on week ends, as most sailors do. It is where we are going to spend the next few years, and we search out all the living and sailing features much in the same way as others do when they select a home ashore. We look at closet space, storage space, bathrooms, day living area, cozy night and cold weather area, cooking and storage facilities, space for guests, bookshelves, and all the conveniences that anyone looks for in a place where he expects to live.

In addition we look for something that I chose to call "integrity" in a boat. This is the construction and design. Is she strongly built? Will she sail well, meaning, have a good turn of speed without too much heeling? Will she survive a strong gale at sea without too much damage? Is the rigging easy to handle so that changing and reducing sail can be done quickly and easily? The older I get, the more important this last factor becomes. Are there lifelines and handholds on deck, and space to move around in as you change sails, and even enough for sun-bathing?

The minute we stepped aboard Elizabeth M we knew she was the boat for us. This same feeling came over me years ago when we were looking for a bigger residence and were led on a parade through house after house. There was one we knew was going to be home as we stepped through the door.

After the broker and owner had led us through the boat pointing out feature after feature, Emily and I went on to the after-deck. I looked at Emily and she looked at me and she said "This is it — right?"

"Right!"

What was it about *this* boat that made it seem ideal for us?

For me, it had a powerful eighty-seven horsepower engine, a big rudder, and a cut-away keel with six thousand pounds ballast and thirteen tons displacement. This translates into a strong powerful hull that will survive most anything that an angry sea can dish out. Dual steering stations meant that we could steer outside on the comfortable after-deck when the weather was fair, and duck inside to the spacious pilothouse when it was foul.

It was a ketch. A ketch has four sails where some

boats have one or two. To get the same high speed the required sail area is divided between the four sails, instead of two — or even one in some atypical designs. Small sails are easier to handle than big ones. In addition, all sails had roller furling, and this made sail handling even more easy.

It had complete instrumentation, including radar, for long distance cruising. All this made the Captain happy.

The Mate was enthralled by the two heads, four cabins, and such things as drawers, hanging closets and good storage for stores. We had the after cabin for our stateroom. The pilot house was large and sunny with big windows. The main salon had a table that could seat six good friends and a galley, including a freezer and cooler. Forward of that was another stateroom for guests with its own head.

The next day we went for a sail as a precondition to our offer to the owners. In a brisk breeze with all sails flying we hit a speed of 6.5 knots (a knot is a nautical mile per hour and a nautical mile is 6080 feet). All the above and a boat that sails well too? We fell in love with her then and there and our offer was accepted.

The rest is dull history, but we didn't move aboard for another thirty days. After all, you can't just kick a guy off a boat in the middle of a foreign country. Before the transfer, the owner needed time to buy a new boat and bring it down to Tortola and transfer his household goods. We agreed to 30 days and then went visiting.

Nothing to do and no place to live for a month seemed like a great chance to get home to Portland, Oregon for a few days, and also to do something about the great cache of goods shipped from Golden Bell in Spain to Emily's brother's place in Pinehurst, North Carolina.

This cache, resting in a storage unit, contained all

the things we had owned while living aboard Golden Bell in Europe for two years. It is amazing how much one can accumulate while living aboard a small boat and one is usually not aware of it until required to vacate the boat. Charts, books, kitchen utensils, clothes, electronic devices, tools, linen and personal items, including Emily's art materials, paints, brushes, sketchbooks and souvenirs, had all been boxed and shipped across the Atlantic. They had made our life comfortable on Golden Bell. We would need them on Elizabeth M.

We went home to Portland, visited with friends, grandchildren and children, got in a couple of days of skiing, and then returned to Pinehurst, where we sorted out the things that we would want on the new boat. Finally, loaded with eight bags, we returned to the Raleigh-Durham airport for the trip to Tortola. We felt that there was no way that we would be allowed to check eight bags, so we decided to try to check three each, and ship two by air freight.

Having shipped two we approached the check-in praying silently that the customer representative would allow us to check one extra bag per person. As it was there was never the bat of an eye when we declared six bags to check, leaving us wondering whether we might have checked all eight just as easily. We landed in San Juan, Puerto Rico and switched to an inter-island plane. This proved to be twelve passenger craft shaped like a box with two pointed ends and a high wing. Emily asked, "Is that what we are going in?"

With a fatalistic shrug we picked up our carry-ons and she sighed, "Oh, well, I'm sure that thousands of successful missions are behind this old bird". None of the other passengers seemed worried, so why should we be?

The plane was full, and we sat just in back of the pilot. There was no stewardess, no lavatory, no "fasten your seat belt" sign. Nothing but pure transportation.

With a good, old-fashioned propeller-generated roar it staggered down the runway and struggled aloft, fighting for altitude. Soon I released my grip on the arm rest, blood returned to my hands, and I looked out the port. Below were a few fleecy clouds and there on the deep blue surface that reminded me of the Pacific, was a tiny sailboat towing its dinghy behind and creating a great "V" on the water's surface. Here was another tropical paradise for the sailor, and, not nearly as far from the continental shores as the islands of the South Pacific. Why hadn't I noticed it when we had flown down to meet Elizabeth M before? Certainly I had not, but, now that this paradise was to be our home it was time that I did.

When we arrived at the airport at Tortola, a very nice customs official had some difficulty coping with our bags full of pots, pans, and other assorted personal items not normally found in the luggage of the average tourist or business person. But, with a phlegmatic shrug, she waved us through and even helped us carry this mountainous pile outside.

There we encountered one of the reasons why the airport at Tortola is quaint. No buses, limos or formal transportation systems exist on the island, just a half-dozen taxis parked across the street waiting for business. A nod of my head to one of the drivers brought him scurrying across the street. Looking at our pile of luggage, he asked, "Is there just two of you?"

"Yes," Emily said with growing excitement, "we're going home."

"Wonderful, welcome home," He said. "You'll have to tell me where you live. I thought I knew most every one on the island, but you must be newcomers."

"In a way, we are. We just bought a boat and are moving aboard tonight. This is our only home."

We decided that we were going to like Tortola. Our driver took us speedily but carefully to the marina. I cringed when he rounded a curve and bluff on the left side of the narrow road, but as we progressed I remembered that this was the British Virgin Islands and true to the twisted but stubborn heritage of that great nation, all drove on the left side of the road. The American-made cars, all purchased in Florida, had the steering columns on the left. I have driven British cars on British roads and American cars on American roads but mixing the two is sporting. It is not something I want to get used to.

We showed the driver around the boat and then sent him off with a healthy tip. Alone in our new home, the excitement began to build. The former owners, Ed and Carrol, had left the boat immaculate and a bottle of Moet-Chandon sat on the salon table with a welcoming note.

With a proper sense of priority, we cracked open the champagne and toasted our new home. One of the household items we had brought with us were two stainless steel wine glasses we'd used to toast King Neptune at the Equator five years earlier, so the toast was made with sufficient finesse.

We settled in quickly and learned to love and sail our new home. We planned to take her up the island chains to Florida, where we will make some modifications. We did not plan to change the name because in the tradition of the sea it is considered bad luck to do so. We flaunted the tradition with Golden Bell, which we changed from Isabel. We thought that maintaining the last half of the old name (phonetically, of course) would protect us. Instead, we were visited with storms of unprecedented strength and duration. Never again!

Of course, we are not the least bit superstitious — but we see no harm in being careful. Incidentally, we have no idea who Elizabeth M was, nor did Ed or Carrol. And, I expect I will be answering many times the question, "If your wife's name is Emily, why did you name your boat Elizabeth M?" I think an arching of the eyebrows, and a stony silence thereafter, should create a whole new mystique.

We enjoyed Tortola and were reluctant to leave but our goal of sailing the great American waterways beckoned us. Several incidents of our stay there stand out. We went sailing on a large catamaran that offered regular four-hour day cruises with a champagne lunch. There was a stout breeze as we motored out of the harbor, and all was serene until they popped the big spinnaker. That cat took off like a startled deer! The captain said that we were doing about 25 knots. The twin hulls were raising rooster tails that stretched back 50 feet. The water close by was a shiny blur. It was tremendously exhilarating.

The next day we attended a style show of mens bathing suits at the marina and the models were the crew from the catamaran. These hunks were a bunch of clowns and we, especially Emily, enjoyed the exhibition very much.

We also attended a garden. Road Town, the principal village on the island, had a park that we had often glanced at but hurriedly bypassed. A local lady in one of the stores had invited us to attend their garden show in the park. We spent a most wonderful afternoon, strolling through well kept grounds and admiring the blooms on display while sipping tropical fruit drinks. Several painters had exhibitions and the artist in Emily feasted. Let me say this about the British. They love to garden, and every where in the world that you find them you will find well tended lawns and gardens. This was true of Road Town which retains much of the British Ambience of 100 years ago. A horse and colt served as lawn mowers in the towns central grassy areas and were occasionally joined by a milk cow.

Tortola is one of the British Virgin Islands and a member of the British Commonwealth and retains much of the British Ambience of 100 years ago. To put things in perspective, a circle of islands sweeps up from the north-eastern tip of South America and terminates roughly at Florida. This circle forms the boundry of the Caribbean Sea. The Northern side of the circle is a chain of islands that includes the British Virgins, the American Virgins, Puerto Rico, Dominican Republic, Haiti, Jamaica, Cuba, and further north, the Bahamas. The Bahamas group sits just sixty miles from Florida.

Nightly we pored over charts planning our routes through these islands to terminate at Fort Lauderdale. There, we would begin our journey up the Intracoastal Waterway and the first leg of our planned adventure.

Our plans were to take a couple of months to cruise up this chain to Florida and then travel up the Intracoastal Waterway to the Chesapeake Bay, where we would spend some time cruising the large number of rivers, bays and creeks of this great transportation resource.

The Intracoastal Waterway is a series of rivers and canals that enable one to travel from Miami to New York city without ever having to go "outside" (in the ocean). It had great military strategic value, especially during WWII when German submarines ruled the Atlantic and the Caribbean. Now it is used primarily by pleasure vessels and some commercial traffic. Since it goes through some very wild areas and some great commercial centers we eagerly looked forward to this experience.

## 2

## *THE CARIBBEAN, THE VIRGIN ISLANDS, PUERTO RICO, DOMINICAN REPUBLIC, TURKS AND CAICOS, THE BAHAMAS*

The American Virgin Islands, just to the west of Tortola were a sharp contrast to the British Virgins. The beautiful harbor of St. Thomas was crowded with cruise ships, and the city was tawdry and filled with gift shops which cater to the disgorged passengers that come in waves, shop frantically, re-board and disappear in the night only to be replaced by another clacking horde. The natives were surly and unfriendly, the town was crowded with tacky houses, mostly occupied by welfare recipients. A customs official said that St. Thomas was the major port for drug activity in the Caribbean and a "bust" was made every other day on the average. In our travels around the world, we came to the conclusion that the U.S. government does the poorest job of helping the native cultures — and at the greatest cost.

One day the customs agent who had become a friend sauntered down the dock where we were moored bringing a young man who had a camera slung over his shoulder. The camera was just a disguise, he said, as they were trying to look like tourists. We greeted the agent warmly and he introduced his friend, another agent. He said that they were on duty and looking for a sailboat allegedly skippered by a known drug runner. The next day we saw that the boat three slips down from us was opened for inspection with all its loose items laid out on the pier. Our friend was there. He and his associate had found their man, but no drugs, we learned later.

While browsing through the shops, Emily had found an art gallery featuring Haitian art. She had always been fascinated by the color and boldness of this distinctive art form. The painting she bought now dominates our main salon on Elizabeth M. It competes for attention with "my" side of the cabin with a bold watercolor I purchased in Spain, and a beautiful conch horn we bought in the South Pacific. So now our bulkheads (boat walls to non-boaters) carried artifacts from the major areas of our travels — the South Pacific, the Mediterranean, and the Western Hemisphere.

One day while we were at the Yacht Haven Marina in St. Thomas I was going ashore on some errand when I was treated to one of those spectacular occurances that seem to bless the lives of world cruisers. Coming toward me on the pier were two people who looked very familiar. As they approached I recognized them as David and Joan Waterhouse from New Zealand. We had first met them in Spain after having talked to them on the Amateur Radio. We met them again at Gibralter where we both were preparing to cross the Atlantic. We aborted our attempt, following a battering by a 10 day storm. We had then loaned them our charts for the western landfalls and the Atlantic.

When I bumped into them they had our charts under their arms and were preparing to take them to the post office to mail to our permanent address!

From St. Thomas we sailed to Culebra. The Virgins are what I would call deep water islands. The islands are surrounded by deep water, but at Culebra we experienced the first of the shallow water islands and reefs. Entrance to the anchorage in the large bay at Culebra was obtained by negotiating a shallow bank that commenced about three miles off shore. By carefully following the well marked channel you are introduced into the large bay. The village of Culebra was charming. We checked in with the local customs, then went exploring. We learned that the hills and beaches to the east were filled with "unexploded ordinance." The U.S. Navy had used that part of the island for target practice for many years. The area contains many beautiful sites for hotels, but because of the danger no one wants to put one up. The Navy, so far, has refused to come in and clean it up.

The next island in our trip up the leeward islands to Florida was Puerto Rico. We sailed there with the ketch Lady Anne. We liked Bill and Frisky Wilder, the owners of

Lady Anne, and, as cruisers frequently do, planned to sail together, a practice known as "buddy boating." Our decision was to sail the south coast of Puerto Rico since it contained the most harbors, inlets, etc. The north coast of Puerto Rico is not as hospitable, and except for the major port of San Juan, and Arecibo there are no stopping places. The south coast, although shallow, has many small anchorages and is favored by cruisers like us who are not in a hurry.

A good stiff breeze favored us all day. Lady Anne being bigger, and therefore faster, was soon out of sight, although we stayed in radio contact. When we arrived at our agreed destination the location of the marina was obvious by the evidence of sailboat masts inside the breakwater, but how they got in there was not so obvious. We plaintively radioed, "Lady Anne, Lady Anne, this is Elizabeth M."

Back came, "Elizabeth M, Lady Anne. How can we help you?"

"Lady Anne, Elizabeth M. We're just outside the Marina but we can't see any way to get in. Can you tell us where the entrance is?"

"Of course, we can see your masts; you are about 100 feet from it."

"Well, I know my eyes aren't as good as they used to be, but all I can see is a breakwater which goes right up to that rocky cliff there on the west."

"Trust us, Paul, when you get to the west end of the breakwater there is an entrance. It is not a wide one, but you can get in — we did."

There was, and we did.

We decided to have dinner ashore. The marina was built in the European style with condos and a restaurant surrounding it. We checked the menu (in French) and the prices (in U.S. dollars). The cheapest entree was $40.00. We elected for a pot luck on Lady Anne. The cuisine (American) was excellent and the price was $250.00 SAVED!

The south coast of Puerto Rico has many charming anchorages, all of which had to be negotiated with care by our deep draft boats. We drew six feet, Lady Anne about six and one half as I recall. Each night, as we met for dinner aboard one boat or the other, we would select the next day's anchorage and agree on a departure time. We visited several quaint villages and were treated to some outstanding snorkeling. In one harbor we took a night tour boat ride to a nearby bay where the photoplankton were so numerous that the surface glowed, and the boat's progress through the water was trailed by brilliant flashes.

Our cruising with Lady Anne terminated on the west coast of Puerto Rico in the lovely, spacious anchorage of Boqueron. The Wilder's were in a hurry to get home and had planned a long non-stop passage to the middle of the Bahamas for the next leg of their cruise. This meant that they would by-pass the Dominican Republic and the Turks and Caicos islands and go directly to Georgetown in the middle of the Bahamas. We, on the other hand, had planned to visit the Dominican Republic meet a friend in the Turks and Caicos and linger for a couple of weeks in the Bahamas.

We trumpeted Lady Anne out of the bay. Trumpeting consists of my blowing the beautiful conch horn we had obtained in the Pacific islands of Tonga. The sounds emitted are sometimes, but not always, beautiful. A conch horn is similar to a bugle in its technical demands, and a bugler has to keep his lips in shape to be melodious. It is traditional to sound the conch when friends leave a harbor and I like to keep traditional, if not melodious.

The next day we crossed the infamous Mona Passage — so designated because of the nasty ride you can have if the wind and current are in opposition. It was an overnight passage and was not too rough, although we entered the Dominican waters in a rainstorm. I navigated by radar from inside the pilot house while the windshield wipers gave me clear vision. Ah-h-h — what luxury!

Samana Bay is a huge indentation in the eastern coast of the island of Hispaniola. The Dominican Republic occupies the eastern half of this large island, while Haiti occupies the western half. The country is very poor, but, a benign government, in contrast of Haiti's, has brought the Dominican's a higher level of living than Haiti's. The Dominican Republic immigration department keeps a close watch on the yachts that come into and leave the country, mostly, we are told, to prevent the natives from leaving on yachts rather than to keep undesirables out. The officials are courteous, but do expect a bribe. The natives are friendly and happy, and the country is verdant and beautiful.

An English-speaking young man by the name of Frank attached himself to us and acted as our mentor all during our stay there. He arranged everything — taxi boats, taxis, immigration, customs and tour guides — and showed us where to eat. He was in his twenties, clean, courteous, and seemed to have a perpetual smile. He was always on the dock, and we always asked for him. Soon the other young men did not bother us and when they saw us coming they would yell for Frank.

The taxis in Samana resembled the pedal cabs of

Hong Kong and other areas of the East, except that the bicycle had been replaced by Honda 100's. When we wanted to visit a nearby waterfall, Frank turned down four cabs until he found one with a new Honda. He was cautious because the route we would take required traveling some distance over some hills, and he doubted that the older models had enough power.

The beautiful bay of Samana had a magnificent arched bridge leading out to a small island in the middle of the bay. It was rumored that the bridge was built by Trujilo for the entertainment of his mistresses. The facts are different, but I like the romantic version best.

We left Samana with a vow to return soon and traversed our longest passage yet, two days, to the island of Providenciales, usually shortened to Provo in conversation and literature. This isle is one of the Turks and Caicos Isles and they are an independent group of islands. Our approach to Provo was our first experience with "bank" cruising. The islands starting from the eastern end of the Turks and Caicos to Florida are characterized by large land masses a few feet below the water. This geological phenomenon, called "banks," and there are many of them, stretch for five or six hundred miles east and south of Florida. These banks are covered with white sand, and you can travel for miles in water that a tall man could wade in. The islands of the Bahamas are small areas that protrude above the water but resting on these vast banks. Most of the villages have some sort of channel leading into them that can accommodate a boat with a six or seven foot draft.

Provo was one such island. To get there we did not aim directly for the village. Instead we navigated to a point about twelve miles southwest of it where the chart indicated six or more feet of water existed from the edge of the bank in to an anchorage near the village. I'd like to say that we soon grew used to traveling for miles, sometimes nearly out of the sight of land, with only six inches to two feet of clearance between our six-foot keel and the bottom. The truth is that we never did get used to it. The charts, of course, indicated soundings but they are not always accurate and depths were not always reliable.

In the shallow water there was another hazard — coral heads.

They grow up from the ocean floor at random , and can be compared to the threat a shark poses for a swimmer. They are hard and rough and can severely damage a boat. You can see coral heads from quite a distance in the incredibly clear water. They show as dark patches, but so does a small patch of sea grass. The usual procedure to avoid them is to station a crew member at the bow of the boat or aloft in the rigging in order to steer a clear path across these watery plains.

We cautiously moved out of the deep water and onto the bank. We plotted a compass course to Provo, but were unable to see it twelve miles away. As we gained confidence in the charts and could suppress our anxiety at being so close to the bottom, we began to look about. We could clearly see fish when we were moving slowly. Real excitement occurred when one or more rays crossed our path. These are dark and nearly square and vary from two to three feet across, although we have seen much larger ones in the Galapagos islands and in aquariums. They move swiftly, but are clearly visible in the clear water against the white sand of the banks.

Gradually Provo rose out of the sea, and about three

hours after we had arrived at the bank, we dropped anchor near the village. The next day we rented a small four wheel drive car and drove to the airport to greet our friend Nancy, arriving from the states. There she was, on schedule and much in need of a tan. This we provided during the next few days with a cruise out to the west of the island where we snorkeled in the incredibly clear water and another trip to the north side to snorkle off deserted beaches. I usually had difficulty getting Nancy and Emily out of the water. I got a little tired and chilled after a half hour in it but Emily and Nancy seemed to have an inexhaustible source of body heat and enthusiasm. I would wait and wait on the beach watching their snorkels bobbing in the water as they floated over the fascinating panorama of colorful marine life below.

What fascinated Emily and Nancy so much is the swarming of underwater life around the coral patches. These patches produce the colorful fishes that can be seen in the pet stores. To see them in their natural habitat and in vast numbers is tremendously exciting. Most have bright colors, some are iridescent and some are very slender and hide in grasses by standing on their tails, and you will occasionally see eels and snakes. The very beautiful fan coral and anemones are sprinkled here and there. My favorite are the tube worms whose brilliant delicate fronds wave gently in the passing currents. Emily and Nancy reported seeing a conch traveling across the sand and hermit crabs scuttling away. There are cautions in this delightful experience. The most obvious is, that because of the wash of water over your back, you don't realize how sunburned you are getting. Another is that you forget the passage of time and can drift a long distance without realizing it.

We kept the jeep for two more days and visited a conch research station at the opposite end of the island. There we learned some fascinating things about the "Queen of the Gastropods." Besides their beautiful shells, conches are an important source of food in the islands, and on the mainland at the better restaurants.

After Nancy had returned to the United States, our next stop was a small bay on the nearly deserted Aklin island. Aklin is the beginning of the Bahamas but is off by itself and not a part of a chain or group. We were now moving North and West toward Florida. Following a leisurely and magnificent moonlit overnight passage, we sighted the island at dawn. From two miles out finding the small anchorage on the almost featureless coast was nearly impossible. We almost decided to give up when we saw a sailboat leaving the harbor. Now, with the entrance located approximately we only had to thread our way to it through the sand bars near the entrance. We were aided by the boat Drummer which hailed us on the radio telling us our sails could be seen. We were asked if we were looking for Atwood Harbor, the name of the bay we sought.

"Drummer, this is Elizabeth M, yes, we certainly are but we can't seem to locate the entrance."

"Elizabeth M, Drummer, we know, we almost missed it too. Can you see our masts?"

"Drummer, Elizabeth M, I think so. It looks like a course of about 160 ought to work."

We tried that bearing, and after a couple of minutes we were contacted again: "Elizabeth M, Drummer, yes 160 is correct. Come on in closer, and we'll tell you if you are getting into shoal areas."

"Thanks, Drummer, here we come."

Twenty minutes later we were dropping our anchor in about 12 feet of water not far from Drummer and one other boat, Swan. This was a beautiful bay: white sand beaches, crystal clear water, and, except for our three boats, totally isolated from the world. We stayed there two days, snorkeling, walking the beaches, and visiting with folks on the other two boats. Drummer left the next day. Kellog and Diana Flemming, the couple on the remaining boat, Swan, were also Commodores in the Seven Seas Cruising Association a world wide association of live-aboard cruisers. Cruising as defined for members means that the boat is your major, or only residence, and that you are traveling, and not parked in a marina somewhere. There are about 5,000 members of the association of which about 600 are Commodores, the rest are Associate members who plan someday to become Commodores.

We enjoyed the company of Kellog and Diana who were just finishing up a circumnavigation. We agreed to continue on, buddy-boating with them up the Exuma chain of the Bahamas. Our next stop was Clarencetown on Long Island where there was a small harbor protected by a breakwater. The sail there was grand, boosted by a brisk breeze. Swan had preceded us, and as we went past the harbor under full sail with the rail down and a bone in her teeth (That's salty talk — translation: we were heeled over and the sea was foaming where our bow entered the water.) we were hailed on the radio by Swan. With a burst of pride I heard Kellog's greeting on the radio. "Paul, you look great out there."

We reluctantly furled the sails and motored in to the harbor and soon had the anchor down near Swan.

The major event while we were at Clarencetown

was the celebration of Emily's birthday at the local and only restaurant. They did not have any champagne, and, since I felt the occasion called for some, I dinghyed out to the boat and retrieved a bottle which we kept for just such emergencies. As we were the restaurant's only customers, we lacked not from attention, and the evening was a merry one.

Long Island was also the first island that boasted a Bahamian customs agent. He had to come from the other end of this long island. He was pleasant, businesslike and hard to get rid of as he wanted to talk to us about our adventures. I think he, too, dreamed of sailing to faraway places with strange sounding names. The village was characterized by two magnificent churches with twin towers, and a blind bartender. The churches were built by a wealthy local salt entrepreneur who switched religions, and therefore had to build a second church to maintain his piousness. It was also pleasant to sit under a tree and drink a cold beer at the blind bartender's tavern. He sat on a bench and talked while you waited on yourself.

Shortly after we left Clarencetown harbor the whole atmosphere seemed to change; visibility grew dull, and a certain ominousness filled the air. Soon the heavens opened up and dumped tons of water on us and some extremely high winds rose briefly and whipped the sea into a foam. Swan was about a mile ahead of us, and, "Karen R" was a couple of miles to our right with owners Fred and Phyllis Fevrier aboard. They had left Clarencetown at about the same time and the three of us had been maintaining radio contact. When the squall blew out about an hour later we resumed radio contact and during the subsequent exchange my heart stopped and my blood turned to ice.

"Karen R, this is Swan, were you guys in that squall?"

"Swan, Karen R, here. No, but we could see both of you just before the cloud opened up and dumped on you. By the way, were either of you chewed up by the water spout that was in the center of the squall?"

Obviously, neither one of us had been, but that was as close as I ever hope to be to a water spout — which is a tornado that sucks up water instead of trees and houses. We have subsequently seen many of them at a distance as this was the season for them.

The spouts are formed when a rain cloud forms so rapidly and releases so much heat that it creates a strong up-draft. Below the up-draft is a vacumn and when this is so strong that it reaches the surface of the water it sucks the water up in it. Spouts can have the destructive force of the land tornados and have sucked boats up in them.

At one time during the squall, the rain was so dense that we could not see more than a few inches beyond the windows. I expect that this was when the water that was being sucked up in the spouts was being dumped. At that time the ordinary windshield wipers were totally ineffective. A rotating wiper on the windshield gave us a clear window out into the torrent. Up until that moment I had seen little need for the gadget.

We followed Swan, rather gingerly, into the Georgetown harbor. The twisted channel was studded with coral heads on all sides. Finally, at a snail's pace, or more appropriately, a conch's pace, we dropped anchor 100 meters offshore from the Peace and Plenty hotel.

The highlight of the anchorage was a visit to a near-by islet which contained the ruins of an old plantation. The gang, Paul & Emily of Elizabeth M, Phyllis and Fred of Karen R, Diana and Kellog of Swan, dinghyed over to it. Phyllis had been there before and knew the way via a somewhat torturous path. She also was a well-informed amateur naturalist and kept up a running account on the flora and fauna, but mostly the flora. Emily and Diana, both eagerly interested in the subject, paused so often to study something that Kellog, Fred and I despaired of ever reaching the sight. The island was overgrown and the mansion was in ruins but with a little imagination the opulence of an era long past could be revived.

Across from Georgetown is a long, narrow island called Stocking Island, and the Georgetown harbor is actually named Stocking harbor. We decided to cross over and anchor in an attractive bay at Stocking island. Swan went ahead as we dallied over taking up the anchor. About half way across we went gently aground with our somewhat deeper draft. The tide was going out and my other-than-energetic efforts to power off soon were of no avail. The water receded. With our boat obviously aground and tilted at an embarrassing angle we had no choice but to await the tide that would rise in a couple of hours. Kellog and Diana motored over in their dinghy to offer condolences and to assure us that we really didn't look as ridiculous as we felt.

A couple of days later we went aground again, about 100 ft in front of the Yacht Club at Staniel Cay. We were swept by tidal flow onto a sand hummock that was only two or three feet under the surface of the water. People came over to offer condolences and encouragement such as "Get a truck!" We passively accepted our fate and joked with everybody. An experienced boater motored over in his dinghy and offered to "take out an anchor" for us. He knew that the only way we could get off was to "kedge" ourselves off. "Kedging" is a process where one takes an anchor out to deep water by dinghy, drops it, and then the stranded boat is winched to its anchor. The anchor catches and holds so that the winching pulls the boat into deeper water. It worked!

After three embarrassing hours we were tied up at the Yacht Club dock. The man who came out to help us said that we were the third boat in a week to end up on that shoal. That helped our wounded pride.

I could continue on with a saga of white beaches, clear water and remote anchorages, but I hate to overuse superlatives. I must add that the passages are tricky and somewhat nerve-wracking. You buy these bits of paradise, but you must pay the price. Along the way, Swan hurried on, and we linked up with another boat that was also flying the SSCA (Seven Seas Cruising Association) flag. Sand Dollar was owned by Charlie and Gini Cohen and, following one another, we just hopped leisurely from island to island, making a few miles a day on our trek to Florida. We ended up finally in Nassau for a few days.

This well-known resort town, with its cruise ships and casinos, is somewhat more sophisticated and not as much to our liking. But, we visited a large casino owned by Merv Griffin and dropped a few quarters in the slots. Emily and I went alone to one of the casinos in the evening, had dinner and enjoyed calypso music. Later we were treated to an outstanding performance on the steel drums. The performer claimed to be the father of the instrument when he discovered that World War II steel drums, left on his island, could be bent and twisted into producing miraculous tones.

In company with Sand Dollar, we spent several more days traveling to Gun Cay. Gun Cay is one of the last places where we would be able to lie quietly at anchor and await the proper weather for crossing the mighty Gulf Stream.

This "river in the ocean" is the most awesome of the many currents that circulate the water in the world's oceans. All of the water of the Caribbean flows north into the Atlantic. It would do this gently if it were not for the fact that it is pinched between the coast of Florida and Cuba on the south and then when it turns north between the Great Bahama Bank and the east coast of Florida. The currents in the Gulf Stream may reach 6 or 7 knots. You must keep this current in mind when you head for a Bahamian island or the Florida coast. Also, if the wind is from the north, a very nasty wave situation occurs which is dangerous to small boats.

Frankly, I thought the Gulf Stream was overrated in its ferocity by timid sailors of the East Coast. They don't know what rough water is really like, I said to myself. With this declaration of bravado, we rose early in the morning and poked our bow out into the full force of the passage. The water remained smooth and calm, the sun shone and the gulls wheeled and cried. A radio message came out of the air, "Elizabeth M, this is Quantro. What is it like out there?"

"Piece of cake," I said, "Calm, sunny, smooth." Quantro had been anchored near us during the night.

"I guess we will give it a try, then. We've been waiting three days for good weather."

Experiencing good weather on a passage is not our usual turn of luck. But, blessing whatever gods were in charge of this piece of ocean, we forged on. We made proper allowance for current and hit Ft Lauderdale on the nose. The four stacks (of a power plant) on the waterfront became visibly close, and we steered directly for them, assuming that we no longer had to compensate for the current. Wrong! Before we knew it we had been swept a couple of miles north of the harbor entrance and had to motor back to the south, bucking a strong current. Finally, Elizabeth M and Sand Dollar motored in to Port Everglades at Ft. Lauderdale in mid-afternoon.

Charley and Gini departed for their home up the Intracoastal Waterway the next day, and we turned to the tasks of finding a yard that could do the repairs and modifications that we wanted. The Bahamas and the tropical isles beckoned us but our plan of circumnavigating the Eastern U. S. was a stronger magnet, mostly because so few had done it. As we worked on the boat, we gathered the charts and guide books that we needed and dreamed and planned.

## 3

## THE INTRACOASTAL WATERWAY, FLORIDA, GEORGIA, SOUTH CAROLINA

Each part of the world where we have sailed has had its fascination. The South Pacific was as romantic as we had imagined. The Mediterranean was equally fascinating but in the sense of ancient history, as we cruised that area we were accompanied by ghosts millennia old. On the East Coast of the United States we were enthralled by the history of our country. A second aspect of our delight was that the Intracoastal Waterway is incredibly beautiful, but in a far different way than most beautiful landscapes.

The East Coast, in contrast to the craggy West

Coast, consists mostly of flat, alluvial plains filled with marshes, sand dunes, low islands and shallow river inlets. The nearly endless marshes seem to stretch from horizon to horizon. Little creeks enter and leave the waterway, and often the Army Engineers have dredged narrow canals to connect the creeks, river estuaries and narrow, shallow lakes that hide behind the sand dunes. The importance of these tidal areas to the life-chain process is now recognized and respected.

The Intracoastal Waterway (ICW) is navigable and stretches from Miami to Norfolk and even up to New England via the Chesapeake Bay, Delaware river, the Hudson River and a short and shallow canal in New Jersey. In all of this distance it is not necessary to go "outside," that is, into the ocean. There is a stated minimum depth of nine feet, except for the New Jersey stretch. When we got to New Jersey, because of our six-foot draft, we had to go outside and harbor-hop up the coast to New York.

The ICW winds its way along the coast using dredged cuts and channels to connect the bodies of water hiding behind the islands and dunes. We often went up large rivers for a few miles and then through a cut down another, and into a large lake where the other end was barely visible. If we strayed a few feet outside the well-marked channel, we went aground!

After we left southern Florida, where the waterway is lined with condo high rises and million dollar homes, we entered the remote marshy areas that were swarming with wild life. The state of Florida forbids the filling in of any marshy areas presently without permission and that is grudgingly given. We have observed several types of herons, most of them snow white. These are the most visible and prolific. Frankly, I think they are stupid! They fly a couple of hundred yards ahead and land. You approach again and they fly ahead again. This can occur five or six times. Sooner or later, usually later, they properly assess the situation, fly off to one side, return and land behind you. We stopped feeling guilty about bothering them so much.

Ospreys we liked. They are numerous and like to build their nests on top of the waterway markers. They make a peculiar whistle if you approach their nest too closely, especially if it has young in it. Emily talked to them a lot, saying such things as, "Now don't get nervous, you beautiful thing. We are just going to whiz right by and not bother you one bit!" To see them dive into the water, talons extended, with a great splash and then mount to the sky with a large fish in their talons, is thrilling.

Our biggest thrill came when we were anchored in a quiet river bend, and an alligator floated by. We had seen many an alligator in "farms," but this was the first we had viewed in the wild. They prefer fresh water and are not often seen in the brackish waters of the coastal streams. We watched as he stalked a beautiful white heron that was fishing in the shallows. He worked his way to within three feet of the heron, taking about 20 minutes to cover the 20 feet. We braced for the rush. The heron kept on feeding nonchalantly. We wanted to scream and scare off the beautiful white lady from the ugly monster. Suddenly, the heron spread her wings and flew about 100 meters downstream. Maybe she was quite aware of the intentions of that old 'gator and had decided things had gone far enough.

On a par with that experience, but of a wholly different nature, has been our manatee events. This mammal has been called the sea cow because it is large, fat and slow.

It browses on sea grass, found on the bottoms of the shallow estuaries. It likes warm, fresh water, so it is most often found in the tidal waters. Manatees are a protected species and their greatest enemy is the high speed motor boat. Because they cannot move fast they cannot escape the sharp propellers which wound and kill. All up and down the waterway we see signs saying "Entering manatee area: slow to 5 knots or less." The local officers who observe violations are quick to arrest and the local magistrates show little mercy. All, including us, are fond of the lovable manatees.

Living on the water, as we do, we have seen more than a dozen manatees. Most non-boating natives have never seen one. The most thrilling experience occurred at the marina at Titusville, Florida. We were watching three of them, a bull, cow, and calf. cavorting and browsing in the marina. The marina attendant strolled over near us, turned on the fresh water hose and directed it noisily into the water. Within minutes the three manatees came over and rolled, played and drank in the hose water. We were able to touch them, and I have some amusing pictures of the cow, lying on her back, with the water running in her mouth and her flippers moving in ecstacy.

We were in Titusville, a village near Cape Canaveral, on August 12, 1989 by design. We wanted to observe the lift-off of the space ship Columbia. The Indian and Banana Rivers, flowing almost due south in central Florida, are kept from entering the ocean by Cape Canaveral. Broad causeways connect Titusville and the rest of the mainland with the Cape and several beach towns. This area is rather heavily settled because of the Kennedy Space Center and the many jobs it brings to the area.

We left the marina the day before the launch and anchored for the night about three miles from the launch site. We were on deck at 0700 the next morning, waiting nervously and sipping our second cup of coffee. At 0830, the local radio informed us that the launch was on the final 60 seconds of countdown. Soon it was "10, 9, 8, 7, 6, 5, 4, 3, 2, 1, Ignition!" There was a brilliant flash, clouds of smoke were thrown upward and the bird was off!! Wow! Seconds later a tremendous vibrating roar of sound washed over us as we watched her climb laboriously into the sky, trailing her totally incandescent tail.

We sat there, sort of stunned, and it was several minutes after the Columbia had disappeared in the blue that we were able to move about with the busy work on the boat. We were rather well informed about launches having been to the Kennedy Space Museum the day before and on a bus tour of the Cape during which we had actually visited the site of Columbia's launch (pad "A"). The silvery "plane" that we had seen mounted on the large rocket the day before was now miles above the earth and accelerating. But, most awesome of all, it contained five or six humans.

Aside from enjoying the wild life and rocket launches we toured many historic sites. St. Augustine, Florida is the oldest city in America. It was established as a Spanish colony by Ponce de Leon not long after Columbus discovered the new world. We spent several days there and were impressed by the city's devotion to its history. Many of the very old houses were carefully restored. Fort Castillo de San Marcos has been fully restored and holds a daily cannon firing that booms out over the yachts anchored below it. Fortunately, we were not one of them. Elsewhere in the city, a typical Spanish home compound is authentic in detail, including a forge, carpenter shop and spinning and weaving operations — all using tools and techniques 200 or more years old. Wendy's, a hamburger chain, is located in the oldest house in town if not in the United States.

On leaving Florida, we went north into the real south. Savannah is very conscious of its history, is very southern, and has a very active historical society. Many homes in the downtown area are restored and, since it is a designated historical area, all property owners — no exceptions! — are required to restore and rehabilitate. The rules are pretty strict and explicit, but encounter little opposition. A large number of the homes are open to the public. Many names from our history books are recorded on the numerous bronze plaques throughout the historic area.

We lunched at an historic restaurant. The waitresses were costumed, and the meal was served family style at tables seating eight. There were no private tables, and the food was excellent. If you lingered too long over your coffee you were asked to leave so the table could be re-set and a new group seated from the long line outside.

Charleston, South Carolina is another city proud of its heritage. You history buffs will remember that Fort Sumter stands on an island that guards the Charleston harbor. Here the first shot of the war between the states was fired (a war that is sometimes referred to as the "Civil War" by damnyankees).

We stood on the ramparts as the park ranger told of that first battle of a long and bloody war. The Union soldiers occupied the fort in spite of the South's demand that they be withdrawn and that Confederate soldiers be allowed to protect their own harbors. The presence of the Union soldiers was an irritating thorn in the South's side. The ranger pointed out a peninsula on the south side of the harbor where the cannon had been set up for the bombardment. When the shells started landing inside the compound, the Union fort commander surrendered. Most loyal sons and daughters of the South maintain to this day (including Emily, born in North Carolina) that the war was about states rights and not necessarily to free the slaves.

I felt so deep in the south in Charleston that I purchased a Confederate flag to fly from our spreaders to signify our neutrality. For the uninformed, when you sail in a foreign country you display a small flag of that country from your starboard spreader as a courtesy.

Charleston maintains a marvelous assemblage of retired naval vessels in a Naval Museum. It includes an aircraft carrier, a submarine, a destroyer and a Coast Guard cutter. The first nuclear ship, the Savannah, a commercial vessel, is there also. All are decommissioned and open to the public. Other vessels, representative of their types, will be added to this floating naval museum as soon as they are decommissioned. We spent a day there, and I would have liked to have spent several more days. I was in the Navy during World War II but had never been aboard an aircraft carrier or a submarine, so I enjoyed the day from a technical point of view. I decided that my assignment on a destroyer escort was superior to an assignment on a huge carrier with thousands of men or the stifling closeness of the submarine. We spent a few days in Charleston evaluating it as a place to leave the boat for the winter. Now that we were out of the tropic waters we could not live on the boat during the winter. It would mean two or three months in our recently purchased apartment in Portland. It was important that our beloved Elizabeth M be left in good hands.

Charleston did not seem to have what we wanted. We continued on north up the ICW. This turned out to be fortuitous. In the next chapter you will learn what it is like to live through Hurricane Hugo.

## 4

### *HURRICANE HUGO*

On the East Coast there is a popular late summer and fall pastime known as "hurricane watching". This involves using a chart of the Southwestern North Atlantic, supplied by newspapers and insurance companies, and listening to the radio each day. We noted the latitude and longitude of the "tropical depressions" on the chart and then track them as new positions are given each day. We carefully listened for two basic conditions on each broadcast: the upgrading from "tropical depression" to "tropical storm" to "hurricane," and whether or not sections of the East Coast are put on "hurricane alert." When the radio said that the

East coast from Jacksonville to Cape Hatteras is on hurricane alert everybody, including us, got nervous because we were in that section. Hugo was still hundreds of miles out to sea and each person listening hoped Hugo would curve enough, or straighten enough, to miss their part of the coast.

When "Hugo," now upgraded to hurricane status and gathering strength, moved south and west in the usual manner of hurricanes, we hoped that it would curve down to the Bahamas, back up to the North, then run out of steam off shore and quietly die in the North Atlantic. This happens to 95% of hurricanes, but every once in a while, one gains in strength and swerves for the East Coast. We nervously watched Hugo as it refused to weaken, grew stronger and stronger, pursuing a straight course for the coast. The local police, stores, the marina, and all centers of activity suddenly started distributing previously printed pamphlets on hurricane preparedness. They were ready; we weren't.

We chose — wrongly we realized later — to remain in the marina, instead of going farther up river and riding it out at anchor. We spent the 24 hours before Hugo struck putting extra lines on the boat and removing valuable and precious things. A local resident of a condominium that was a part of the condo-marina complex had invited us to store our things in his appartment and spend the night with him. We gratefully accepted.

The next task was to give Lizzie a fighting chance by tying her securely to the pilings. Emily was off somewhere, but I cut a ¾ inch anchor line into short pieces and I used them to secure Lizzie to the pilings and walk-ways of the marina. During the process I fell into the water and gashed my hand. Normally this would not be worthy of mention — in fact, I studiously avoid alluding to such incidents. In this case, I make an exception for the following reasons.

When we first arrived at the Belle Isle marina just south of Georgetown, we were much amused by a sign at the head of the dock that, among other rules for guests said, "DO NOT FEED THE ALLIGATORS".

"Very amusing," I said, "Great PR".

A couple of days later we saw a small three-foot alligator floating near the headwalk. A couple of days after that a fat, humongous 12-foot alligator crawled out to sun himself on the mud flat about 60 feet from our boat. When I fell into the water my life did not pass before my eyes — only the vision of that big old 'gator swam before me. I could have outswum Johnny Weismuller racing to the ladder about 20 feet away. (Those born after WWII wouldn't remember this intrepid Tarzan Hollywood star who outswam and outfought many a crocodile in the Tarzan movies of long ago.) When Emily returned she insisted that I go to the emergency ward to have my hand stitched up. I didn't want to take the time, as Hugo was closing in on us and the winds had already started to build, but you can never win an argument with a wife or a doctor, and Emily is both. So we went. Six stitches and two hours later we were back at our boat and loading our possessions into the car. With a stiff upper lip we bid Lizzie goodbye.

We went to Ben's condominium and carried our possessions in to the relative quiet of his house, and we settled down to monitor Hugo's progress on television. We heard there was to be a mandatory evacuation of Georgetown. However, we decided to stick it out with Ben because his condominium was on relatively high ground.

Although the wind had already built up to 50 or 60 knots we were not too worried because the greatest threat to the coastal communities during a hurricane is not the high winds, but what is called the "surge." The surge is caused by the winds piling up the water on the shore. It is usually only a few feet and will cause little flooding if the surge comes at low tide. If it strikes at high tide the flooding can be deadly. The reports had been that only a five or six foot surge was expected — but it was expected at high tide! We still thought we would stick it out but we did move what we could to the second floor. The TV Station went off the air. We began to get nervous.

A police car went by with loud speaker blaring "Everyone is ordered to evacuate this area and proceed to the nearest hurricane shelter!" A neighbor came over with a radio report of a 12 foot surge. We and everyone else climbed into cars and headed inland.

The first shelter listed in the handout was full. The second, about 10 miles further had been turned into a headquarters for police and auxiliaries. The third building a few miles further was a school and was not yet full. The winds were now about 60 miles per hour or better. We three were the last ones admitted. It was 9:00 P.M. We joined 347 others grouped or sprawled around the two large rooms, the assembly hall and gymnasium. I was amazed that so many were asleep sprawled on the hard floor without mattresses. We alternately dozed with our heads on our arms and talked.

Once we were startled awake by a commotion and some yelling over in a corner where some teen-agers had congregated. The cop who was stationed there walked over and things quieted down quickly. That may have been because a man who had gone in and out of the storm a cou-ple of times was told that he would not be allowed back in if he left again. He didn't believe it, but the next time he went outside he stayed. I liked that cop. He also evicted a couple of teenagers for smoking, since smoking was against the rules.

_ About 4:00 A.M. I tried stretching out on the bare floor, realizing, of course, that I could never sleep. Two hours later Ben shook me awake, saying, "It's light. The storm's over. Lets try to make it back to Georgetown."

Emily, Ben and I dodged downed trees and power lines on the return trip and made it all the way except for the last half mile, where downed trees blocked the road. That short distance seemed to be more heavily devastated and we speculated that there had been a tornado spawned by Hugo. The great live oaks had branches torn off, some of which had lodged against condos. A fascinating phenome-non occurred in some of the autos that had been left parked there — they had windows out, usually the back window or the windshield. We decided that this was further evidence of a tornado. This was consistent with what we had noted that several of the windows in cars at the shelter had exploded outward. We had seen this in the parking lot of our shelter when we had been allowed to go outside for a few minutes while the "eye" of Hugo passed through.

We walked back to Ben's. Although there were many huge branches about, most of the trees had survived. Some had leaned into buildings and we could see the dam-age that some of the larger branches had caused. It was like a scene out of a horror movie with trees and wires down, and windows broken. We stopped briefly at Ben's condo-minium which had been little damaged, and then walked the rest of the way to the marina. I was fearful that we would find Lizzie on the bottom, or worse, high and dry on the land.

As we rounded a bend in the road we could see masts in the air, and with leaping heart we saw among them Elizabeth M's distinctive ketch rig with radar dome.

Emily screamed, "Paul, Paul, there she is! See, she has to be floating or she wouldn't be sticking straight up!"

As we stood on the shore, she looked OK. Other, closer, sailboats appeared to be floating as well. Several motor boats had sunk at their moorings, and the piers and walkways were utterly devastated. Not only were large sections gone or in shambles, but the entire northern floating section had just disappeared. Everything carried a heavy load of marsh rushes that had been uprooted by the storm. The two fuel tanks had floated up out of the ground, and a leak in one was dumping diesel fuel into the river.

With the walkways destroyed we had to find a small boat to get out to Elizabeth M. We found our dinghy and motor, that we had left ashore tied to a post. The dinghy had been deflated and the pump to inflate it had been left on the boat. We found a skiff and launched it. It leaked but we paddled out to Lizzie using a scrap of board as a paddle. There was damage to the railings and a few scratches, but she was afloat! Most of the damage had occurred because the boat next to us had broken loose and battered the railings. Ten of the twelve lines with which I had secured her had chafed (worn) through. Inside she was dry as a bone. A few dishes were on the floor but only one was broken. We spent the afternoon cleaning and checking and bringing the things back aboard that we had left at Ben's. We were amused when he invited to share a can of soup for lunch, and found that with the electricity off his only can opener was an electric one. High tide would be necessary for us to get out of the marina due to a shallow entrance, and the next high tide would not be until morning.

We could have stayed at the Belle Isle marina and repaired and cleaned things but we were depressed by the devastation around us. Boats that we thought undamaged started to sink. There was no way to get to shore except by dinghy. Our dinghy motor was inoperable. The town had no electricity, some telephones worked, most didn't. There was a run on the few small grocers who had re-opened. The super-markets, who are so dependent on computers and automatic door openers, were closed as were most other businesses. Looting seemed confined to a few small areas and was not heavy even there.

I returned the car we had rented, telephoned my son in Portland and gave him a list of others to call who might be concerned about us. We inflated the dinghy, loaded the outboard motor aboard and rowed back out to Elizabeth M. With the dinghy in its davits we were ready to quit this scene of devastation and continue our journey northward. Soon we would call the insurance company and get Lizzie M restored to her beauty, but now, we just wanted out of there.

We left on the morning tide and dropped anchor behind an island up the river about 10 miles. The next day we went farther up the river to one of our favorite places on all the East Coast-Buckport. It was isolated, and full of real country folks. There was a fine restaurant. We purchased a small outboard motor and explored some of the creeks that went way back into the swamps. We tasted the best sausage we have ever had. Its memory haunts our tastebuds to this day. We would like to have stayed there for a week or two but we needed to make Elizabeth M whole. We moved on to Southport, North Carolina which had adequate repair facilities.

Once we had Elizabeth M out of the water and ready to be worked on, we drove up to Baltimore and rendezvoused with our cruising friends Don and Rhoda Bosley. We sampled the delights of Baltimore in their company, enjoying the spectacular water front, the Aquarium, a concert, and a drive into Pennsylvania Amish country. We also drove down to see the Annapolis Sailboat Show considered to be the world's largest and finest. We returned to Southport via a drive through Shenandoah valley. The fall colors were just forming, but the experience was still breathtaking.

Filled with euphoria we drove into the boatyard wondering what changes had occurred to Lizzie. The answer — zip, nada, nothing!

We had expected the work to be half completed by the time we returned because the yard management had promised us that it would be finished in two weeks. With a discouraged sigh I trudged up the stairs to talk to the manager. My complaints were sympathetically received, but little action ensued. I knew then that I would have to spend the next two or three weeks bird-dogging the job so that Elizabeth M and her crew could return to their natural element — the water. There was another reason we were discouraged.

Life afloat has problems, but life ashore on a boat has many more — some of a very frustrating nature. You must go up and down a shaky ladder, you cannot use the head, you cannot use the kitchen sink to wash dishes and vegetables, noise and dust are prevalent and privacy is almost non-existent. We had two weeks of this facing us, probably more if the manager continued to stonewall our work. Daily I trudged up the stairs to his office and grew increasingly upset. Men would start a job and then disappear for hours on another job. I finally found out why. The secretary said, "Those jobs are from the boss (the owner who was in another city) and you can't expect us to put your job ahead of his, can you?"

This called for sterner measures, "If that job cannot be completed by next Monday (7 days)," I said,my voice shaking with anger, "I want our boat put back in the water and we will find another yard who keeps their promises. You tell Dale (the manager who was not in) that if he can't make and keep that promise I want to know now!" An hour later Dale came out to the boat and promised that the job would be done by next Monday.

Well, it was, almost. On Wednsday his people were finshed and there was only the painting to do. This took three days and then the sign painter had to re-letter Lizzie's name and touch up a few other spots. One month after we arrived there, Lizzie went back into the water.

Once back in the water we moved on north to Pamlico sound still searching for a good winter storage. A small yard and marina at Minnesott Beach on the sound proved ideal. It was well protected, from both wind and waves, the owners were conscientious and friendly. Two of our friends in the area gave high marks to their skill and dependability. Lizzie had found her winter den.

This was the first time we had had several months away from the boat since we had started cruising five years earlier. We made big plans for this free time. If all went well, Emily would participate in a painting seminar, we would do a lot of skiing, and, we would visit the Galapagos!

The latter plan was eagerly anticipated by Emily and I since we're both very fond of observing wild life, and when we sailed to the Marquesa islands in the Pacific, we considered the detour to the Galapagos too far out of our way. Now we would see these unique, historic islands.

# 5

## *THE GALAPAGOS,*

For the past 5 years we had lived on our boat in tropic climes. Now, back in our own country and embarked on our grand adventure in areas where the winters were fierce, we had to leave the boat. Sure, some do live on their boats when winter winds howl and snow piles on the deck — but they will admit that the life is hard. Now with Elizabeth M snugged down on the "hard" we flew home to Portland for three months.

With all this time to spare we took advantage of it to buy a pied-à-terre, a nest, where we could seek refuge. We had generally returned to Portland only for a couple of weeks around Christmas time to be with friends and family. But now we would be home more frequently and for longer periods. Yet we had no intention of giving up the cruising life and our dream to travel the canals and rivers of America.

A condominium was the answer. We just shut and lock the door and leave when ever we want to and for as long as we want to. We have no lawn or shrubs or flowers to arrange for and no pets, and when we return we just turn the key, air it out a little, and we are home! Our neighbors are never sure whether we are home or off somewhere in the world. You cruisers and wannabees, sell your homes and get a condo if you want to be free — and isn't that why you go cruising in the first place?

Once we had found our pied-à-terre we flew to the Galapagos. When we sailed to the South Pacific we wanted desperately to go to these islands where Darwin is supposed to have first realized the principles of natural selection. They were 500 miles out of our way and we had heard that cruisers were not very welcome there — in fact, were allowed only a three day stay, and sometimes not even that.

There is only one way to describe our visit to the Galapagos — Incredible! We went on a package tour, the only way to go. The Ecuadorians want desperately to maintain the purity of these islands, and to visit them you must have a guide and you must observe their rigid rules.

If you enjoy wildlife you will not be able to duplicate the Galapagos experience anywhere for the simple reason that the animals and birds there have no fear of man. We stood within two meters of blue-footed boobies watching the mating ritual. We have swum in a clear lagoon with fur seals who vied with each other to show us how fast they could swim, or how high they could jump. Emily and I were snorkeling and watched a courting ritual between a pair of seals. They were slowly rotating, head down and rubbing noses in the clear water. We observed male frigate birds with their bright red chest pouches inflated as they vied with each other for the attention of a female perched on a limb near by. We handed a twig to a female red-footed booby sitting on a nest who calmly accepted it and wove it into her nest.

We stayed at the Galapagos Hotel the first two days before we went aboard the motor yacht that was to be our home for a week. Iggy, our favorite iguana, a male of no small proportions, habitually sunned himself on our concrete veranda. The entrance and exit to our cabin-like unit was frequently rather precarious as we stepped over or around him. Once he seemed a little annoyed, but most of the time we were completely ignored.

Our two days at the hotel at Academy Bay, on Santa Cruz Island, enabled us to enjoy a morning with the giant Galapagos turtles. These huge creatures, weighing several hundred pounds and looking like large round rocks, were dotted all over a grassy hill. Having been exploited by man, they were timid and withdrew into their shells if we got closer than five meters. They were a favorite source of fresh meat to the whalers, and other passers-by until fairly recently. The practice was to stack them in the hold of the ship upside down. They would survive for months on no food with only an occasional bucket of water thrown on them.

Onboard the yacht we visited most of the islands, accompanied by a natural historian-guide who took us on hikes and snorkeling trips and explained and identified the birds and animals that we saw. There were other passengers on the yacht and a crew of four. We were a congenial and interested group whom the guide said would rank up in the top five percent of the groups she had guided in her several years of service. Jose, the cook was a jewel, preparing excellent meals under difficult circumstances. They were wholesome but not gourmet. The guide, Yvonne, really knew her geology and biology. She was a lovely woman and tears came to her eyes, and ours, when we parted. The Captain inspired our confidence, and the other two able seaman were helpful, cheerful and unobtrusive.

As a special favor, the Captain took us to a lagoon that was literally swarming with sea turtles. Several were observed mating (I'm glad I'm not a lady turtle) and many swam under the panga (small boat). A special delight was a formation of golden rays that swam by near us — not to mention a couple of sharks. The captain also took us to meet his parents on Floriana Island. We hiked a couple of miles inland and spent an hour chatting and having tea with them. Their modest home consisted of a collection of buildings intermingled with plantings of tropical flowers and shady trees.

We flew back to the real word with its forces pulling us this way and that. Whenever these forces become overwhelming, I remember the tranquil life of that lovely couple on Floriana.

## 6

## PAMLICO SOUND, ALBERMARLE SOUND, DISMAL SWAMP CANAL, CHESAPEAKE BAY (SOUTHERN HALF)

When we returned to Elizabeth M at Minnesott Beach, North Carolina the owners of the yard told us that they had had four inches of snow that winter, the first they had had for twenty years. This was not a big deal to us but it was to them. They apologized and said that they didn't think it had harmed Elizabeth M. Of course not — she is a tough lady! They proudly showed us a picture of our boat capped with snow. When we arrived she was back in the water and we went aboard with the feeling of returning to an old friend.

We contacted our friends in the area, including Dave and Joan Waterhouse who had wintered on their boat Psyche in New Bern about 20 miles farther up the Neuse River. They are from New Zealand and our paths seemed destined to cross frequently. This is not uncommon among cruisers, but the incident in St. Thomas combined with others before and after do make it seem that they are part of our destiny. The weather was still a little stormy but we, Psyche and Elizabeth M, decided to test the Spring weather with a short cruise out to Ocracoke, a small village on the outer banks of North Carolina not far from the infamous Cape Hatteras. It had a small harbor and a fascinating history.

The present inhabitants still spoke a dialect that was difficult to understand. Two hundred years ago their ancestors prospered by looting the ships lost on the reefs of Cape Hatteras. It is even rumored that they misplaced lights to confuse the sailing captains so that they would founder on the reefs, and some even say that they refused even to aid in the rescue of the people onboard the vessels. The truth is conveniently lost in the mists of history. We wanted only to drop anchor in their harbor on a pleasant cruise for one night.

We met Psyche at Oriental a small town on the Pamlico sound and also the home of our mutual friends, George and Margaret Madgewick. George and Margaret are expatriates from Australia who still maintain a bit of the Australian accent. Dave and Joan have a lot of their New Zealand accent. Dave claims that New Zealand is the only place in the world where English is spoken without an accent. I, of course, maintain that it is in Nebraska.

George and Margaret, whom we first met in New Zealand had left North Carolina several years ago on a circumnavigation on their beloved Bunyip, a pretty and seaworthy sloop. When they completed their circumnavigation they built their home in this sailing-oriented community.

Following a delightful evening at George and Margaret's we set out the following morning for Ocracoke in a strong breeze. We had a fine sail but the wind built all morning. Soon it had reached 25 to 30 knots and some gusts were gale force. It was quite evident that winter was still hanging around. At about 11:00 A. M. while Emily and Joan were talking on the radio they expressed concern about our choice of harbor for the night. I don't know about Dave, but I was relieved when we all agreed to find a safer harbor. You see, we macho guys hate to admit that we'd like to chicken out.

Accordingly, we changed course for a well protected anchorage up the Bay River. There we found quiet refuge from the spring tempest and good holding for our anchors. The next day we moved over to anchor in front of a small village and dinghyed ashore. We took a substantial walk and drank in the peace of this almost totally isolated community. Emily, with her knowledge of this area said that along Pamlico Sound and especially out on the banks there are many such communities that have changed little during the last century.

Two days later the wind abated and we had a much slower but more pleasant sail back to the New Bern area. There we parted with Psyche while we visited other friends at Fairfield Harbor, a few miles east of New Bern. Janet Claman, one of Emily's best friends, was visiting her cousin Ellen Pringle, who lives at Fairfield harbor with her husband Bob. They own a sailboat and cruise during the summer with their yacht club. Janet had never sailed and was looking forward to the experience.

We motored out of the harbor for a while, then a slight breeze caused us to put up the sails. Janet saw boating as a way to enjoy the sun on the deck and had brought a book to while away the time. She and Emily spent most of the morning lounging on the foredeck and chatting. The mild breeze grew into a strong one and finally it approached 20 knots. We occasionally got Lizzie up to 7 knots — about as fast as she can go. We were well heeled, and Bob and I were having a great time trying to coax a few more tenths of a knot out of her.

Emily finally approached us with a suggestion that, "Janet might be frightened by this speed and heeling and couldn't we maybe reduce sail just a little bit?"

I looked forward to where Janet was lounging, still immersed in her book, and apparently unconcerned. I said, "Well, maybe a little bit but not too much because Bob and I are having such a good time."

We took the sails down as we entered a narrow channel in the middle of the river. We passed a sailboat anchored off to one side. As we did, the lone occupant stood on the bow and signaled that he was in distress. This signal for distress is made by standing raising the arms above your head and crossing and uncrossing your arms.

We quickly cut the engine returned and anchored near him. He needed some fuel, as a fuel line break had drained all of his fuel into the bilge. We tried but were unsuccessful in pumping fuel out of our tanks. We took him in tow with a long line and agreed to tow him into Fairfield Harbor. All went well — until we went hard aground! We knew that there was a shallow spot near the entrance but Bob had said that we would miss it if we headed straight for the entrance. Things got pretty interesting when we stopped suddenly but the boat we were towing didn't. At our previous speed of four knots, it just keep on going. The skipper steered around us as he went past, but he reached the end of the tow rope and swung around dramatically. We got off the bar with our engine, went on into the harbor and our tow cut loose at the fuel dock.

Later Emily said, "You know, that was one of the most exciting sails we have ever had and I suppose Janet thought it was normal.

"I don't know whether we have cured her of sailing forever or whether she liked it. She certainly didn't scream or seem too agitated."

"I guess we should have asked her," I replied, "On the other hand, Henry (her husband) is not a sailor and not really the type so, since she survived this episode, I doubt if there will be any more."

"Yea, maybe your right," she said, "Let her think it is normal. It does make us look sort of 'swash-buckling', doesn't it?"

David and Joan left the next day after our return from our joint cruise and headed on up the waterway, destination Annapolis, Maryland. We had stayed to visit at Fairfield Harbour. In Annapolis they planned to sell their boat and return to New Zealand. We saw Psyche several more times and spoke on the radio once. When we finally arrived at Annapolis, they were there and had not yet sold their boat. One evening when we accidentally shared the same anchorage Dave said, "I have heard all around the world that Americans were kind of rough and unfriendly. I can't say too strongly how untrue that is. Some of the nicest people we have met anywhere are here, especially on the Chesapeake."

My heart glowed at that remark. I guess we really are a nation of friendly people, and not at all like we are painted by politicians and activists in many countries. We have run into a number of "Yankee, go home" situations around the world that left us with a feeling that nobody loved us and that perhaps it was justified. It is not.

Cruising further up the East Coast put us in touch with some beautiful, wild scenery. As we left the vast swamps and low country of the Carolinas we become more involved with rivers, lakes, and sounds. When we were on rivers they usually are principally northerly and we followed them only for a short distance to avoid being led too far inland. Then, perhaps a cut, which is a long canal, would take us into a lake that was just behind the outer banks. Always we were surrounded by the wilderness of the swamp, or wound through cypress groves. Occasionally we passed a small village, but generally our only contact with civilization was a distant house.

After we had crossed the Albermarle sound, about two-thirds of the way up the Carolina coast, we entered one of our favorite rivers — the Pasquatank. Part of the reason we liked it was because its resident village was Elizabeth City. Some years ago a couple of water-oriented residents (probably retired shrimp trawlers) decided that they wanted to make Elizabeth City the best known stopping place for pleasure boats on the Intracoastal Waterway. The waterfront was improved and made attractive. There were slips for transient pleasure boats and the first two nights were free. Residents appeared late every afternoon with refreshments for the tired travelers. A volunteer drove up in his car, opened the trunk and displayed wine, beer, soft drinks chips and several kinds of cheese. We also took a walk and strolled over the bridge that would be raised as we traveled on north. The bridge tender was standing outside his cabin, and we stopped to talk. He was a proud young man and felt his responsibility strongly.

The next day after we arrived, we rented a car and drove over to Kitty Hawk. This historic site of the first flight of an airplane was on one of the outer banks and, at the site of Orville and Wilbur's adventure, there was a museum containing an exact replica of that first plane. What was most impressive was the story of that effort. The Wrights researched a great deal and the principles of flight that they discovered are still used today in the design of our advanced space vehicles.

The trip up the Pasquatank was a totally different adventure as we wound through an endless cyprus forest. The feeling was that the forest just had to be teeming with wild life. Unfortunately, other than the usual plethora of birds we saw only one snake. We had seen one small deer earlier in the month. In fact, the story went that a cruiser asked a villager if there was any wild life around here. "Only on Saturday night," he replied.

At the top of the Posquatank we entered the Dismal Swamp Canal, a part of the Dismal Swamp Wild Life Sanctuary and operated by the National Park Service. We locked up into the canal and wondered what delights awaited us.

The Dismal Swamp is neither dismal nor a swamp. The canal is lined with well tended fields. It is also overhung with trees that have grown up and overhang the canal.

We had to keep in the center as we moved along to avoid entangling our rigging in the branches.

It was a calm sun lit day and the trees were reflected dramatically in the water. About half way through the canal we came upon the information center. It was new and there was a fine jetty where we tied up. Popular fable says that George Washington was the surveyor of the canal. The truth is that he was one of several investors in the canal and did some advising on its construction, nothing more. We were allowed to stay there overnight and it was a peaceful night.

The next day we finished our transit of the Dismal Swamp Canal and moved into the metropolitan area of Norfolk, Virginia. We passed mile "O" in the center of Norfolk. From there the miles are measured southward down to Key West. These mile markers are important when we were moving along the ICW to locate our position. Every five miles in most areas there would be a pole stuck in the shallow water designating the number of miles south of "mile 0" we were. By knowing exactly where we were, and knowing our speed we could decide where we would be about time to stop for the night. Passing Mile "0" therefore was a great mile stone (or should I say more correctly "mile buoy") to us on our northward voyage. There would no longer be mile markers and a direct route to follow.

We were about to enter the huge Chesapeake Bay. Where our radar, Loran, and compass would be used frequently. Another important instrument would be our eyes and Emily greatly out-shines me in that skill. She can spot a buoy and suggest a change in course long before I can convince myself that it is really there. Well — I am five years older than she!

The earliest settlers rather heavily populated this rich and fertile area, and some towns date to the 16th century. Many rivers legendary in our country's history flow into the Chesapeake. These in turn are fed by other rivers and broad creeks. It is said that you could cruise there a lifetime and not drop your anchor twice in the same place. It has only two drawbacks — the Chesapeake is shallow so you must navigate carefully, and it is filled with crab pots. These latter, pesky things consist of a metal cage which rests on the bottom and is attached to a float on the surface with a strong line. If one of these lines gets caught in your propeller, it can ruin your whole day. The watermen and boaters have learned to live together. Crabbing is allowed only in certain areas but that includes almost everywhere except in regularly traveled areas.

We were astonished by the Naval ships in the Norfolk harbor. It is certainly true that Norfolk's principle industry is the Navy. There were several floating docks, all but one containing a Naval ship. There were several huge carriers and other ships of massive bulk whose purpose was mystifying to this old Navy salt. The largest of the submarines were there as was the battleship Iowa. The aircraft carrier Coral Sea was decked out in bunting and banners and the crowds of people around it signified that some thing big was going on. We never did find out what.

We anchored in the Poqueson River the first night and in the York the second. The York was filled with fish traps. These are made by stretching netting between stakes driven into the bottom. As the fish swim up or down the river they are herded by the net into a closure from which they cannot get out. Men come out in small boats and scoop them up. Obviously the traps work only in shallow waters, and this was a characteristic of many of the rivers.

The York also is the location of Yorktown where the decisive battle of the Revolution was fought. An hour at the fine museum there followed by stroll through the battle field gives you an "A" in American History.

While leaving an anchorage one morning who should come out of another branch but Psyche. We talked on the radio with them and arranged to meet in an anchorage farther up the bay. They were headed for Annapolis, but did not want to get there and sell their boat and then regret not having enjoyed the Bay. That afternoon we rendezvoused in the Coan River at the mouth of the Potomac. The next day, after radioed good byes to Psyche we crossed the Potomac to the entrance of St. Mary's River. The Potomac near its mouth is a very large river. I doubt if even Superman could have thrown a dollar across at this point. We would like to have gone up the Potomac to Washington, DC but it was 90 miles up there and 90 miles back. We felt a little pushed because of our decision, now strongly held, to do the complete circle back to Florida. We would have to sail the Great Lakes before fall became winter.

We wanted to go up St. Mary's City for two reason's. First was that we had heard that it was a beautiful old town and that you could anchor right off the St. Mary's college and their beautiful and very old campus. Secondly, we had talked to the secretary of the Westsail Owners Association, George Bachman, whom we wanted to meet. We had known him for years while we owned two different Westsails (a brand of boat). We spent a pleasant evening with him and an enjoyable night in this most pleasant of anchorages.

Two anchorages later we again ran into Psyche.

Perhaps I should mention that her hull is a strong red. We saw them passing far out on the bay and talked with them on the radio. I should also mention that Psyche is a fast boat, much faster than Elizabeth M. The wind had come up strongly, and Psyche was really plowing a furrow in the bay. So were we. All sailors know that all it takes to have a sailing race is two sailboats on the same body of water. We couldn't keep up with Psyche and they soon radioed that they guessed they would go on to the Choptank since they were making such good time.

We headed across the Chesapeake for the Choptank the next morning and soon had enough wind to fill our sails. We had a grand day of sailing, as we never dropped the sails until we entered Broad Creek near our planned anchorage. Broad Creek empties into the Tred Avon river and this empties into the Choptank River. The Choptank was made famous in Michner's Chesapeake, but you will look in vain for the island that is central to the theme. One of our most pleasant evenings was spent on Broad Creek. It was calm, and apparently remote. The mocking birds sang in the trees on the shore and a whippoorwill called from a nearby field.

The next day we moved over to Oxford on the Tred Avon River. This is an absolutely charming town with an Inn that is very old. Not far down the main street is an ice cream parlor. We bought cones and went across the street into a park that fronted on the river and watched the sailboats go by. There are many very old houses and a stroll through these quiet streets is very rewarding. A couple of days and a couple of anchorages later we entered Annapolis and went up Back Creek to our destination — Bert Javin's Boat Yard. We passed Psyche anchored in the middle of the stream but their dingy was gone and there was no one aboard.

We spent a couple of weeks working on the boat, touring Washington DC, and enjoying the company of Joan and David. We rented a car which helped us to get things needed for the boat and to drive in to Washington for the tourist bit. It was about 60 miles but we drove only about 40 miles to the beltway and took the commuter train in from there. Dave and Joan joined us and, other than the usual awe over the monuments, etc. were much impressed by our system of government. Their native New Zealand has a unicameral (single body) legislature.

Our greatest thrill occurred during the graduation of the naval cadets. The Blue Angels, the precision naval flying team puts on a show for the cadets. Every one who has a boat is out on the Severn River to watch this show. It is claimed that you can walk across the river stepping from boat to boat. Since neither David or I wanted to take our boats out in that kind of crush, we decided to take a lunch and dinghy out. We took our dinghy since it was bigger and it was an inflatable, packed a lunch and refreshments and set out the mile, perhaps, to the site. The press of boats had been exaggerated, but not a lot.

The performance of the Blue Angels was magnificent to the point that I, who have flown a little, did not believe what I was seeing. After about an hour of performance we all (several hundred boats) started to return. It was pleasant sharing this experience with our friends. It was a great party and I was proud of our country and its fighting forces.

We also went down to Mt Vernon, George Washington's home, with Joan and David. We truly enjoyed their company. Their plan was to stay there in Annapolis and continue to try to sell their boat. If successful they would buy a car, fill it with their possessions, and ship it to New Zealand. We learned later that they were unable to sell Psyche so they sailed her home to New Zealand and sold her there. They are now growing Kiwi fruit on a farm they own. They are both registered pharmacists but decided to farm rather than set up another pharmacy (Interesting play on words there.) Having spent so many enjoyable times with these lovely people it was a pretty tearful occasion when we said good-bye and headed on north pursuing our quest.

During our stay in Annapolis, Emily decided to take a sailing course to bolster her self confidence at a school called Womanship. On the "T" shirts the women wore was the motto "NOBODY YELLS."

I swear I have never yelled at Emily — well maybe a couple of times — in our six years of cruising. Most of the women held her in awe, considering her world-wide sailing experience, but, in a true sister fashion, understood her need to sail without the domination of her husband.

Someone once stated that it seems that you spend a lot of time in the repair yards. This is true. But, like most things in sailing, it is relative. There is one truth in boating: the more luxuries and gadgets you have on board the more time you, or someone, spends fixing them. Elizabeth M did have a lot of gadgets. I suppose we could have spent most of our time repairing them, as we did with our first and second boat. I am quite mechanical and have been able to fix most anything with some professional help. Now that I'm older and retired, it is quite a strain on the old salt to hang upside down in the engine room fixing something.

We have met young couples around the world who are completely self sufficient and sail on a shoe string. We also find that they have a simple boat with no frills. No air conditioning, no freezer or refrigerator, no electronic gadgets, and a simple stove. They navigate with a sextant, they listen for radio weather forecasts on a simple receiver, they do without fresh foods on the long crossing. Some even sail the world with no motor, not even an outboard! They only go into a yard to haul out so that they can paint the bottom with a fresh coat of paint. Some even skip that by going up a river where there is a large tidal difference and "careen" the boat for painting the bottom. Careening is going up at high tide on the beach, waiting for the tide to leave you high and dry, and painting fast before it comes back in.

Here is a list of what we did at Bert Javin's:

1. Re-rigged the main sheet for easier handling from the wheel position.
2. Installed main sheet traveler control.
3. Inspected all standing rigging and furling equipment.
4. Had radar checked and adjusted.
5. Changed freezer compressor belt.
6. Checked alternator and several other electrical problems.
7. Made up and installed an amateur radio antennae.
8. Install horn button on after deck.
9. Repaired mainsail.
10. Filled propane tank.
11. Installed shelves in forward head.

These are all small jobs, not vital to the success of our cruising. Numbers 1 and 2 were convenience oriented.

Number 3 should be done every chance you get. Number 4, I had a technician do because as it turned out the reason I was getting poor images was because the radar was badly out of tune. Number 5, the belt was only worn a little bit. Number 6 was the principal reason I had selected a yard. Several times I had had a dead battery — but fortunately we had more than one battery. Number 7, just an improvement over the existing antennae. Number 8, something that I had wanted for a long time. It cost little but took time to install. I did it myself. Number 9, essential to get that repaired before it split all the way across. Number 10, routine. Number 11, greater efficiency and storage.

So, we didn't really have to repair anything except the mainsail, but I'm glad I noticed the rip in time. Besides, I had no lawn to mow, no walks to shovel, no dripping faucets to fix, etc. etc. Did I mention that all the two weeks we were there we got free moorage in the boat yard?

Finally we were ready to start up the Chesapeake and on north toward the Hudson.

## 7

## UPPER CHESAPEAKE, NEW JERSEY, NEW YORK
## THE HUDSON RIVER

We had enjoyed our visit to Oxford on the Choptank so much that when my nephew and his wife accepted our invitation to visit us on the boat, we back-tracked 50 miles in order to meet them at Oxford, MD. As we entered the Choptank we were fortunate enough to observe some skipjacks at work in the river. Originally the skipjack was a flat-bottomed sailboat used for oystering in the Chesapeake. Now, they have been replaced by motor-boats. Well into the Choptank there is an area rich in oysters that can be harvested only by the skipjacks and then only once a week. Motors are prohibited in this oyster bed and harvesters must sail out and back. Several skipjacks towed dinghies with motors on them but I assume that they could not be used except to get home if there was no wind. We were fortunate to have passed by on this special day and it was a great thrill to see this great cloud of sails clustered on this special bed.

There is a lot of sentimental attachment to the skipjack and I suspect that this special day and this special bed of oysters have far greater sentimental value than commercial. Several times a year the owners of these fine vessels gather for races and over mugs of beer bemoan the loss of the good ol' days. Sailors do a lot of this.

The Ice Cream Parlor was the first place we went with my nephew, Bob Cox, and his great bride, Peg Stermer. He is in computers, and she is a first lieutenant in the Army. She radiates intelligence and authority in a petite, feminine fashion, and I predict rapid promotions for her — that is, if competence still counts in the services. She had been transferred to the Washington area for further training, making possible this visit. After consuming our cones we dinghyed out to Elizabeth M, and settled down for a few days of relaxed cruising. We were happy to have this opportunity to spend more time on this most interesting peninsula.

Oxford is about midway down the peninsula which is shared by Maryland, Virginia and Delaware. The peninsula is without major industries, or ports, and the inhabitants are mostly farmers who farm in the same fashion as their grandfathers. The watermen who live there harvest the rich marine life of the Chesapeake Bay also in much the same manner as their ancestors, except instead of sailing and rowing they now move about with outboard motors.

Watermen built many craft designed solely for use on the Chesapeake. The skipjacks were one of the designs. The hull of the skipjack is box like with a flat bottom, a centerboard, and a bow sprit. The flat bottom enabled it to work in shallow waters and kept it from tipping too much as the oystermen worked their rakes at the rail. The boats were generally gaff-rigged and many had two masts. (A gaff is a boom on the top of the sail. Its purpose is to increase the sail aloft. They are not used much in modern designs.) When the boats had gathered their bounty for the day, the sails were raised and the skipjacks raced back to sell their load. Those who got there first got the best price.

Many other boats were designed for the Chesapeake, all smaller than the skipjack. All had shallow drafts and nearly flat bottoms. Many of the old designs are now equipped with motors, but little changed otherwise. Several museums honoring this romantic past exist around the Chesapeake. One of the best is in the village of St. Michaels on the Eastern Bay, Maryland. There you will see an old Chesapeake Bay Lighthouse, a fully rigged skipjack, many of the smaller working boats, a complete workshop where new boats are constructed in the old way, and an exhibit of the very large shotguns, mounted on skiffs, that were used to slaughter waterfowl for the markets.

As you sail through certain areas of the Chesapeake, you wonder how there could be any crabs left in the bay. Many areas of the bay are so densely sown with crab floats that it has been necessary to designate channels so that both pleasure and commercial boats can live together. At one point, I became confused as to our location and started through one of these heavily sown areas. Dodging crab pots would not be difficult if the floats were easy to see. Some are. Some aren't. A choppy surface makes all of them difficult. As I mentioned previously, you don't want to get them tangled in your propeller.

The first two or three pots are not so bad, but we were headed into a vast area that I thought would soon clear. Wrong! About two hours later, dripping perspiration and with blood returning to my knuckles, we burst out into a cleared channel. That was the last time I disregarded Emily's advice to turn back.

Well — almost the last.

In parts of the bay there are designated "crab free" channels leading to marinas, towns, and, of course a roadway for the large ships. All these zones are shown on the charts and we learned the hard way to read the charts before setting out. These channels benefit both the pleasure boater and the watermen. Crab pots are expensive and without the channels the larger boats would just ignore the pots and chew them up in passing and the smaller boats would be denied free access to vast areas of the bay.

The Tred Avon River which feeds into the Choptank, has many charming anchorages along its course and in its headwaters. I was happy that we had a close encounter of the wild life kind while Bob and Peg were aboard. Two large white swans and eight cygnets came over to visit us while we were anchored in a pretty bay. They had an established routine of visiting all the boats that anchored in the bay, about six when we were there. You could see the swan family approaching majestically toward your boat, a whole flotilla, and you frantically searched for slices of bread to feed them. What a magnificent sight! As the day wore on and the swans repeated their visits, our attitude changed from being charmed to "The bloody beggars are back." The cygnets had reached about half of their growth and were covered with a ragged coat of pin feathers mixed with emerging adult feathers. We did what we could to help them achieve full growth, even though it did short us on breakfast toast.

We reluctantly returned Bob and Peg to Oxford where their car was parked. Their presence on our boat had brightened things considerably. It is good to know that our armed forces are still attracting some of the "brightest and best." We sent them off with many hugs and returned to Annapolis for provisioning.

That finished we proceeded north a short distance to Gibson Island. We visited with Bill and Frisky Wilder, who live there and whom we had last seen in Puerto Rico. It was a thrill to motor into their bay and see their ketch, Lady Anne, moored there. We had last seen her as she sailed out of Boqueron Bay on the west coast of Puerto Rico.

We now moved on north up the Chesapeake Bay, feeling a little pushed by the calendar. There is genuine winter up in the Great Lakes area where we were going and we wanted to be past that segment of our journey when the winter storms commenced. So we pushed on. We went through the Chesapeake and Delaware Canal and down the Delaware River to Cape May, New Jersey. We could have gone further up the ICW had we not been hampered by a six foot draft. There are many places in the stretch of the ICW up New Jersey where the depth of the Waterway is only four feet.

So we exited the Waterway, after waiting a couple of days due to high winds out on the ocean. We can handle rough seas, but don't deliberately leave a port when there is a storm if we don't have to, and, since we are retired, that is never. We paused at Atlantic City to pay tribute to Donald Trump's "Taj Mahal" (garish!) and managed to leave with more quarters than when we arrived.

One phenomenon which will remain with us for a long time was the "nightly dance of the seagulls." The tower of Trump's Castle was illuminated by powerful flood lights that projected on up into the sky. In this cone of light, hundreds of white seagulls soared and dived and whirled. It seemed almost cosmic, and it went on all night long!

Our first stop in New York Harbor was at Sandy Hook, N. J. then across to a marina in the Garden State. As we passed under the Narrows bridge we knew we were really in New York! There, in the bright morning sun, stood that gorgeous green lady that thrilled so many of our ancestors — the Statue of Liberty! We motored over close and took some pictures as the sun glistened off the folds of her robe and she saluted us with her torch. Then we moved on to Ellis Island, where those same undaunted ancestors were herded like cattle full of hope that soon they could set foot on the soil of the feisty young republic. We just couldn't enter this harbor in a small boat without thrilling to these ghosts of the past.

We cruised past the Battery, awed by the World Trade Center towers and the jungle of Wall Street. As a Boy Scout, 53 years ago, I had stood in the Battery Park, gazed out at the scene and romanticized coming into this harbor on a sailboat. I guess we need to keep our dreams alive and seize the moment when we can realize them — even if it takes a half-century! I think, as Emily and I had discussed this sailing in the Eastern U.S. a couple of years ago, my decision to decide to do it was strongly influenced by those dreams and those memories of 1937 when a half-dozen Scouts from Ainsworth, Nebraska journeyed to Washington D.C. to participate in the first World Scouting Jamboree.

We were a little uneasy about cruising on up the Hudson, thinking that there would be few marinas and places to stop until we were many miles up the river. We dodged a tanker and a tug or two and hurried on up past 57th Street — frequently thought to be the center of the universe. We nodded to the Chrysler Building and waved to the Empire State building. These icons of New York had stood the tallest and proudest 50 years ago. Now we had to search carefully to pick them out of their more massive (but duller) neighbors. When seen from the water the city sounds were muted and the hustle of the city was not apparent. The buildings shown in the morning sun, monuments to man's enterprise.

The sparkle of the Big Apple is in it's brownstones, Central Park, the theaters, Broadway, the arts, shops, restaurants and hotels. These were hidden from us in the mass of glass and concrete. Our close-up was of abandoned and rotting piers. A hundred years ago this harbor teemed with activity. Ships from all over the earth were tied to bustling piers while cargos were unloaded by sweating stevedores. Around 54th street we passed a few piers still in use. One housed an aircraft carrier, the Intrepid, as well as a submarine and two tour boats. One of the tour boats was the Queen Elizabeth II. The carrier housed the Intrepid Maritime Museum.

The view soon changed to Riverside Park, and huge apartment complexes. Soon we saw a small opening, the Harlem River, which connects with the East River and signifying the end of Manhattan Island. The palisades of the Hudson now began to express their grandeur. Moving at a surprising rate, we proceeded up into the Catskills, under bridges and over tunnels connecting the teeming millions of New York to the New Jersey shores. Yet, except for an occasional multi-story apartment house, we saw little evidence of the people, just trees and water.

Our speed up the river was due to the fact that we were riding the "tidal bore." This phenomenon we had used to advantage once before when going up the Seine River in France. A tidal bore results when slow-moving rivers empty into the sea. As the tides rise and fall on the ocean due to the moon's gravitational influence the water actually flows up river. If you catch this movement just at the turn of the tide, you can ride the wall of water, the "bore," up the river. Instead of slowly bucking a current up the river and making slow progress, you can actually move at a high rate of speed adding the speed of your boat to that of the bore. We had, unknowingly, caught the bore.

We finally arrived, late in the afternoon, at the Tappan Zee and found a marina just beyond the Tappan Zee bridge. Ah! Shades of Washington Irving. We re-read the Legend of Sleepy Hollow over evening cocktails in order to get in the mood of this scenic area of the Hudson. It succeeded. All night long I rode Tartar through the woods, hurling pumpkins at the hapless Ichabod Crane (With a little help from one of Emily's delicious stir frys. I think it was the second helping that did it.).

Upstate New York, which we penetrated via the Hudson, is quite mountainous by Eastern standards with peaks of 2,000 to 4,000 feet with names such as "Storm King," and "Bear Mountain." On one of these Rip Van

Winkle dozed away a couple of decades.

The Hudson has few twists and turns as it heads north. West Point is on one of the few bends of the river. I had never been able to pinpoint it geographically in my mind, coming as I did from a small town in Nebraska where any place east of the Mississippi was the "East," and "not New York City, or New England," but in another dimension of time. The Army cadets train on a beautiful campus hidden from the river by stately trees. Just a few of the taller and more massive buildings gave evidence of its presence. Some magnificent old houses showed on the bluffs, probably those of the senior officers.

On we went, up through this legendary country, surrounded by water and trees, to Catskill-on-Hudson. The guide book had listed the Hop-O-Nose marina in "Catskill" as one of two places on the upper Hudson where our masts could be lowered and laid on our deck. The transit of the Erie canal necessitated this because of many low and fixed bridges.

While our masts were being lowered the workman brought an elaborate plywood support to hold the front end of the masts at the bow end. I told him, "I hope I'm not paying for that," I told him, "A couple of 2X4's will do the trick."

"Oh, don't worry, you are not paying for it," he said, "Some one a couple of years ago had it built. Just leave it at Wardell's in Tonawanda. It has come back through twice already this year. We may see it again before the season is out." Wardell's Marina at the other end of the canal was where we had planned to have our masts raised.

The Hop-O-Nose marina was named after a famous Indian of the local history. The marina was about 200 yards up a quiet creek. It had a fine small restaurant, and a swimming pool. The people were very friendly and cooperative. We would like to have lingered there but we were anxious to get into the Great Lakes before their all-too-short sailing season was gone.

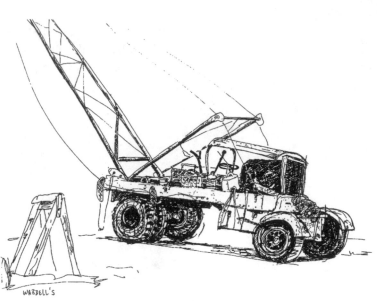

WARDELL'S

## 8

## *THE ERIE CANAL*

Until we entered the Erie Canal, New York State
seemed pretty much as we expected it to be. The great
sprawl of New York City followed by the majesty of the
Palisades; the romantic Catskills reviving memories of
childhood verses and legends; the magnificent estates peep-
ing from among the trees, and the jewels of Albany and
West Point; all combined and conformed. But when we
turned our bow inward to cross northern New York State
we had not expected to be so isolated from the bustle of a
great state. Of course, those of you who have been with us
for the last five years (see Sailing the Golden Sea) know

- 78 -

that we are not strangers to canals, having toured France through its canal system. Other than the basic mechanics of canal touring, the two experiences were vastly different. France has many ancient historical sights, compared to our country, such as villages cathedrals, and castles which date back many centuries. The French canals wind through heavily tilled fields and forests and trees are a rarity. Their canal system was in place long before we began our first canal here in the New World.

All canals that were dug before the invention of the internal combustion motor have the mule path at their bank and the Erie is no exception. Today, however, it is used by cyclers, strollers and joggers. The mules walked this path connected to the barges by rope. A portion of each barge was given over to the mules welfare. It contained feed and a sort of stable. There were usually two mules one rested while the other worked. Both French and American canals formed the major commercial highways until the middle of the 19th century when railroads began to compete. Except for bulk commodities today's commerce has pretty nearly abandoned this slower form of transportation for trucks and railroads.

The first lock was on the Hudson at Troy, which is just a few miles past Albany. We locked up only a few feet. The lock keeper gave us some literature and asked us if we were going on the "Erie," or on up to the "Lake," meaning Lake Champlain.

The lock keeper said that we ought to go up to Champlain the next time. "Good sailing," he said. He told us that in 1775 Lake Champlain was the scene of our country's first naval battle? Benedict Arnold fought and destroyed a British fleet there and gained a much needed year for our emerging republic.

"Lots of history up there," he said.

Emily, who is much more gentle with such people than I, replied, "We promise that the next time we pass this way, we will take time to go to Lake Champlain, but, right now we are headed for the Mississippi and have to get through the Great Lakes before winter."

This seemed to impress him so, without another word he handed us an additional folder which was a description of the Erie Canal. He said, "Just hang a left about half a mile up the river." And we did.

We waited in a park-like setting for the first lock to open. Eventually it discharged a couple of power boats. Incidentally, by the time we had travelled the entire length of the Erie Canal we realized that we had not seen one commercial vessel. When we commented on this to one of the lock keepers he said that the only significant commercial traffic consisted of a few barges in the fall carrying corn and corn oil.

Two locks later we locked up into a quiet pool above a low dam. It wasn't really quiet, however, because there was a state park just across from the quay to which we were tied. We had decided to spend the night there, but were beginning to regret the decision because of the presence of several jet skis. One performer got his thrills from aiming for us while standing facing the rear of his small craft. I gradually relaxed as his skill proved that he really could steer the darn thing backward safely. I had never felt that we were in danger since Elizabeth M outweighed his craft a hundred fold. At sun down they all went home and peace reigned again.

At that time we were just above a device called a

"gate" on the navigation charts. In all of France we had seen only two such devices, and those were in the swampy areas of the Camargue of the southern coast. Their purpose is still obscure, although one of the Erie lock keepers explained that they protected the canal. To my query, "From what?" he answered that he didn't know. He supposed it was from the ice in the winter, or something. These gates are huge heavy steel doors that lower into a frame in the canal and block off the canal. We saw 20 or 30 of these in the length of the canal.

Although we were officially on the Erie Canal, we followed the Mohawk River as it wound through upper New York State. We would have felt isolated from civilization had it not been for an occasional cabin, along the shore. The channel was well buoyed and as long as we paid attention, we were in no danger of grounding. Once or twice a day while on the river we would go through a lock that raised us above a dam. These dams slowed the current, deepened the channel and tamed the rapids.

Locking through these locks was quite sporting. Although the lift was usually short, the lock keepers sometimes, perhaps on purpose, filled the locks at a rapid rate which caused strong swirling currents in the water. These pushed and pulled our boat sideways, forward and backward. The lock keepers in this the eastern section seemed to care little about the problems of pleasure boaters. They would not take our lines, saying that regulations prohibited their doing so. I found their attitude curious since there was no barge traffic, and the canals were open primarily to accommodate the pleasure boaters. We were forced to hang on, almost desperately, to the ladder rungs that were inset into the walls. These were rusty and poorly placed. To cap the ignominy, when you were locked up to the top you were greeted by a sign that said, "Do not moor to the ladders." The signs are ignored by both boater and lock keeper. The grounds around the locks were neatly kept and the locks as a whole were kept in good operating condition. Nearly all of the keepers were courteous and friendly.

But, the lock keepers of the western half of the canal were more friendly. They had secured ropes to the bollards at the top that dangled down into the cavity and had covered them with plastic tubing to keep them from becoming a slimy mess. These we could grasp and keep our boat from being tossed about by the incoming water.

We would enter an empty lock slowly and pull alongside a ladder. Emily would lead a bow and stern line through the rungs of the ladder to provide us with a tenuous mooring. Behind us the gates would shut with a clang, followed by a much louder clang as the water pressure forced the gates to seal and lock. Most lock keepers then let the water in slowly so that the swirling currents did not buffet us about. This made it easy for us to keep the boat steady since we were essentially moored by only one line at the middle of the boat. I stayed at the helm with the motor running in case the lines broke or Emily was unable to hold Lizzie M against the strong current. The swirling currents subside as the volume of incoming water decreases compared to the volume of water in the cavity. Soon the lock was full and we would motor slowly out into the canal with a friendly wave to the lock keeper.

Only once did we approach disaster. At an early lock the water came in very rapidly. The bow of Elizabeth M began to swing out. Emily screamed, "I can't hold her!" I grabbed a boat hook and from my stern position tried to straighten out the boat by pushing against the wall of the lock. I turned the rudder, hoping that would help and was about to tell Emily to cast off and we would take our chances in the middle of the lock.

By then the lock keeper realized his error and quickly choked the flow of water. With the reduced flow, we could get Lizzie under control, and peace reigned once more in the lock.

Our impression of the state of New York was vastly different from the city. It is green, substantially forested, and inhabited mainly by placid cows munching grass and an occasional hawk wheeling overhead. As we moved west we saw less cornfields peeking at us behind the tall river grass and more barns and silos. This sylvan scene was frequently blasted as the freeway or railroad curved in to the edge of the water. When long freight trains sped down the river and huge trucks roared along the highway, it was easy to understand why the canal was no longer used by commerce.

As we have seen in other countries and would later in the Mississippi watershed, bulk cargos, such as grain, coal and sand, are still moved by barge. The canal holds few traces of the great commercial highway that it once was. Such towns as Albany, Syracuse, and Rochester grew to become cities along the canal. Others, such as Brockport, Spencerport, Fairport, Middleport, and Rome, born to serve the canal, were unable to grow as the railroad assumed much of the hauling chores. It is interesting that they were located about the distance apart that a mule could plod in a day. These once prosperous towns now consist of huge old houses and quiet streets lined with old elms, oaks, and neat beds of flowers. To stroll along them is to stroll through history. This we did as often as possible.

Our travel day was as follows: if we got up early we could make about 40 to 50 miles in a day; if not, we could make only 20 or 30. We would breakfast, and I would start the engine soon afterward with my second cup of coffee in hand. Emily would untie the boat (or raise the anchor), coil the lines and put the fenders in a locker. As soon as the mooring lines were free, I would engage the motor and ease slowly out into the center of the canal. Then increasing the RPMs enough to give us a speed of five or six knots, we would begin each day's adventure. After sniffing the morning air and casing the surroundings (and checking to make sure I wasn't going too fast), Emily would go below and do the breakfast dishes. Later she would relieve me at the wheel or just sit on the afterdeck and watch the landscape unfold. She would check the guide books, and we would select a potential stopping place for the night. Thus we passed our days on the canal. Our distance was affected by the number of locks we would meet, or, as in the western part, the number of bridges.

The western part of the canal was rather a long stretch and, since we had reached the same height as Lake Erie there were no locks. The afore mentioned bridges were for cross roads. These bridges were only one or two feet above the water, but could be raised six or eight feet. Before raising the bridge the bridge keeper would ring a bell to announce the event and then lower the barriers and raise the bridge. We decided to record this ceremony on our video camera when we reached the last bridge. For some reason this final bridge had no bell.

Lunch was always prepared and eaten under way. Sometimes Emily would feel like cooking a gourmet meal, sometimes I would feel likewise. I consider myself a pretty good chef but, admit to a limited repertoire. Sometimes it was peanut butter sandwiches. We normally stopped about 3:00 P.M. This gave us time to relax, have dinner, a stroll through town and mentally re-create the bustle of days long gone.

In one such town, St. Johnsville, I was carried back to my childhood by a confectionery. A confectionery, my childhood chums would know, is a place where you buy ice cream sodas, jelly beans, and lemon drops. The boys entered in groups and the girls in groups, and there was a lot of giggling and blowing the paper covers off the straws.

As we left the supermarket we observed an Amish couple come out and board their buggy, pulled by a beautiful, glistening black horse. The buggy was shiny and their faces were shiny. The teen-agers were absorbed in each other. The horse did all the driving while the two laughed and giggled over their ice cream cones. The horse was street-wise, halting at the stop sign, waiting for traffic to clear and then stepping smartly out into the right lane. Could this be a solution to our highway carnage? Teach horses to drive?

Another memorable stop along the way was made at Ilion, about a third of the way across the state. This modest town is the home of Remington Arms. We toured their factory, both Emily and I having been trained by our fathers to shoot. As you might expect, the factory fascinated us as we watched many small parts being made and the whole coming together in a shiny new shotgun. We walked corridors with guns stacked on carts. We saw small parts being made whose function was a mystery. We saw stocks being made in the "stock" room.

We paused before the entrance to one room, where we could only stand in the doorway and watch. It contained robots that busily tended machines. They followed lines painted on the floor and moved from machine to machine. I presumed that the reason we could not go in there because they did not brake for humans. They passed boxes of blank parts to their cousins, called milling machines, which accepted them and after performing operations passed them on to another "servicing" robot who took the box to the next machine, and so on. It was a bit eerie. Emily, on the other hand, was more impressed by the collection of old guns and paintings exhibited in the factory museum. Those of you who are old enough to remember will recall the fine paintings that were commissioned for Remington and featured in their advertisements in outdoor and hunting magazines. They usually depicted a camper or cowboy, threatened by a vicious beast and reaching for his trusty Remington. These scenes were a part of the romantic drive I acquired as a boy in the dusty plains of Nebraska as I devoured copies of Outdoor Life and Field and Stream. I had no interest in going to heaven. If I had a fly rod, a trusty horse, a Remington and a ten gallon hat — I would already have reached that place. Upper New York State is dotted with "finger lakes." These are formed of gouges in the land, probably created during the last ice age. They are many miles long and only a few miles wide. All, including Lake Champlain, are oriented in a North-South direction. These, too, were trade routes of the past and three of them, Seneca, Cayuga, and Champlain, are connected to the Erie canal. Other lakes — Onieda, Cross, and Onandaga — were, at one time, part of the canal system. One of our regrets while transiting this great waterway was that we would not be able to spend years exploring it.

The romance of the period, roughly 1825 to the turn of the century, is well described in a novel Rome Haul, by Walter D. Edmonds. During this period the canal teemed with barges. To serve them towns grew up to service the heavy traffic. One enjoyable event that persists to this day was called "Canal Days." For a few days once a year the canal was shut down for a great celebration. There were booths, tents, special entertainers, lots of food and drink, carnival rides, and all those other good things that make people happy. That tradition of the canal has not changed and we were fortunate to be traveling on the canal when these celebrations were taking place.

We encountered a "canal day" celebration as we entered one of the smaller towns. We wondered why the colorful tents lined the canal. We stopped, discovered what was happening, bought some cotton candy, and continued on. We arrived later in that day at our destination — the town of Tonawanda. The canal was covered with pleasure boats, one line moving slowly in one direction, and on the other side, another line moving in the opposite. Ferris wheels and other rides whirled in the downtown area and brightly striped tents and awnings housed concessionaires. We could hear bands playing. The smells of cotton candy and popcorn drifted across our deck.

We proceeded to our planned stop (Wardell's) the only local boatyard where, we had been told, we could have our masts placed back in their proper position. Since we were about to enter the Great Lakes and there were no more bridges to pass under, we hoped to sail as much as possible. Finding the yard was not difficult, but docking was impossible. We shouted to the owner who was busy at the gas pump. He asked us to moor on the opposite side of the canal until he could clear a place for us.

That was no problem, except for a constant stream of small boats going in opposite directions up and down the canal. We waited, maintaining our position, for about 15 minutes for a gap in the lines. None appeared. In the code of the sea there is a principal of right-of-way called "Tonnage." It provides that bigger and heavier vessels have right-of-way over lighter, smaller, more maneuverable vessels. Since most of the boats in both lines were much smaller than ours, we decided to just barge our way across. As soon as I saw a solid line of small enough boats coming I just stuck the bow of our boat into the middle of the stream of boats. They paused, respectfully I like to think, to let us through. The line in the opposite lane also parted, and we reached the opposite bank. Our objective had been obtained mostly through bullheadedness on my part — for which Emily declined any responsibility. We tied to the wall and strolled into town to join the revelers.

The next day our masts were hoisted up by a home made crane operated quite well by Mr. Wardell, the owner of the yard. He was a loquacious individual who had made all of his equipment out of scraps and was quite proud of the fact that he was referred to by the townspeople as the "MichaelAngelo of the Junk Yard." He spent about an hour touring the yard with us, describing in great detail each piece of equipment and the source of the scraps from which it was made. Mr. Wardell's fame had spread, and even back on the ICW we were warned that he was "interesting" and "could talk a leg off of you." He was contemplating retirement and planned to sell the place in a few years. It occurred to me that in 100 years or so, he will be a part of the colorful history of the Erie Canal. Perhaps the voyage of Elizabeth M will also be a part of it.

At Tonawanda we entered the Niagara River, where we traveled a short distance to Buffalo. As we traveled on the river I tried not to think of the falls just a few short miles down stream. At Buffalo we entered the Black Rock Canal and Lock which skirts the Niagara River Rapids that curve around the north side of Tonawanda island. As you might suspect, these rapids can move you rather rapidly to a spectacular view of the falls from the top in case your engine quits.

Here at Buffalo we entered the first of the Great Lakes — Erie.

9

*LAKE ERIE, LAKE ST. CLAIRE, LAKE HURON, THE*
*NORTH CHANNEL, STRAITS OF MACKINAW*

Cruisers, such as ourselves, set objectives in the form of areas where we want to spend a large amount of time. For example, when we left the South Pacific our next cruising objective was the Mediterranean, where we wanted to explore and spend time getting to know the area and the people. When we left Buffalo, N.Y., our next cruising objective was the North Channel Islands, a wild area on the northeast part of Lake Huron. This area is also at the north end of Georgian Bay. Georgian Bay is almost another Great Lake, were it not for its wide exposure to Lake Huron. We were looking forward to cruising this area which is dotted with hundreds of islands and channels that border primitive wilderness where moose and bear are frequently seen. We also planned to meet Emily's cousin Liz and husband Ted there for a week or so of relaxed cruising.

We left Buffalo after sampling a tasty tid-bit, popular in the East, called "buffalo wings." It is a very spicy, deep fried, chicken wing. My opinion? If buffalos did have wings they would be jet propelled.

The southern coast of Lake Erie is relatively featureless, so we had planned only one stop, but this did not mean that we would not put in to harbors for the night. We stopped at Ashtabula, a lovely name, Erie, the city, and Dunkirk, which has a familiar ring to those of us who knew WW II. At Erie we did not go into the city but to an island and a state park called Presque Isle. There was a nice bay with plenty of water, wildlife (mostly swans), and quite a lot of happy people as it was a weekend. We spent a pleasant afternoon writing, painting and fixing.

The next day was one of a brisk wind and low visibility, our radar was not working. When we arrived at a planned stop in Cleveland we then had two bits of business. One: Get the radar fixed. Two: Get the door for the forward head. Oh! don't most heads (toilets to you) have doors? Yes, but the former owner of Elizabeth M, who lived in Cleveland, had removed it because it had opened awkwardly, and there was another door that completely closed off the forward compartment. But, the door was ours and we wanted it! We called the owner's telephone and the woman house-sitter, who is minding the house while the owner is off cruising in his new Grand Banks Trawler, brought the door down. She was an attractive young lady and brought an equally attractive friend with her. We spent a delightful hour chatting with them. Oh, yes, we got the radar fixed, too.

As soon as the radar was fixed, we left for Kelly's Island — one of several at the east end of Lake Erie. We could not get the anchor to set (dig in and hold) off the island so we moved in to a little dock and store where the friendly proprietor welcomed us.

Our next stop was Leamington, Canada, where we telephoned in our presence to the Canadian customs officials. There in a modern marina we had our engine controls repaired by a fine mechanic who had plans to sail around the world soon and was going to earn his way by repairing boat engines. Leamington is a quiet town of modest size but has two outstanding features: They proudly proclaim that they are the tomato capital of the world, and, it is the home factory of Heinz tomato catsup. That is all nicely logical. A local taxi driver reached down into a sack and handed us a couple of the largest and reddest tomatoes that either of us had ever seen.

Our travel up the Detroit river was, as you might suspect, rather awesome as we slipped mile after mile past large industrial plants and finally past the spectacular city center. In the process, we passed our first of the huge ore carriers that ply these lakes and several foreign cargo vessels. The connection with the seas of the world is through the St. Lawrence river.

Soon we passed the spectacular and beautiful Renaissance Center, surrounded by other attractive buildings of the central city. Emily had attended a medical convention there years ago and had pleasant memories of the Center. Beyond, we passed the Grosse Point area, where the homes of the auto greats are located, and the Grosse Pointe Yacht Club. We toyed briefly with the thought of stopping at the Yacht Club, perhaps for lunch, but there was not enough time left since our objective was to cross Lake St. Claire before nightfall. Incidentally, we have been received warmly by yacht clubs all over the world.

If we had stopped there we might have met a lot more "Gosh People." This is my term for the people who, on a Sunday afternoon, stroll down to the docks to see the pretty boats. When they ask us if we are really from Portland, Oregon, they respond with "Gosh!" We didn't run into too many of these on the coasts where world cruisers are not such a rarity. But here in the heartland of America we were a novelty of sufficient status as to justify a "Gosh!"

The Detroit River connects Lake Erie with Lake St. Claire, which is connected to Lake Huron through the St. Clair River. This smallish lake appears to be an after-thought when the huge ice-age glaciers scooped out the Great Lakes. As we crossed it numerous shoals and rocks kept us alert, but we avoided disaster by staying in the well-marked ship channel.

When we first saw this white smear on the horizon , we couldn't comprehend what it was. As we got closer the "smear" separated into swarms of dinghy-size boats filled with determined men and women — many in their teens. There must have been 400 or more, all of nearly the same size. We carefully skirted the fleet and pushed on into the St. Claire River.

In Sarnia we lucked out again. The Kellers may not do too well on weather, but they seem to do very well on festivals. In Scotland when we bought Golden Bell, we attended a Highland Games Festival at a village close to the shipyard. Here in Sarnia we again attended a Highland Games Festival with competitors of international stature.

We also witnessed a new event in the games that we had not seen before — the throwing of the Haggis. Haggis is a Scottish dish that is generally described as "pretty awful." It consists of oatmeal and the worst of the "awful" from slaughtered pigs. The only good part about it is that most Scots wash it down with tumblers of scotch whisky. A frozen hunk of haggis which is, I presume, of a precise size and weight, is thrown by women standing on a half barrel. The one who throws it the farthest is, of course, the winner. I never did find out who won, but it didn't seem to matter much. I had my money on the four-year-old who just barely got it off the barrel.

Sarnia has a beautiful waterfront park where the festival took place, and the marina was a part of that park. As you can suspect, we took our leave reluctantly after two days of the events. We had 200 miles of Lake Huron before us before we arrived in Mackinaw City, and we needed to be there on Labor Day. Emily's cousins, Ted and Liz Young, had arranged time off from their business in New Hampshire for that time.

The trip up Lake Huron had a few interesting moments. Both Lake Huron, on the U.S. side, and Lake Michigan have, about every 15 miles along the coast, "harbors of refuge," and they are so designated on the chart. I asked at a chart shop in Sarnia why they were called "harbors of refuge" and not "marinas" or "ports." The answer was "If you have ever been out on Huron when a nasty thunderstorm pipes up, you wouldn't have to ask." Waves as high as 73 feet have been recorded. That is almost twice as tall as Lizzie's mast! The two dangerous features of Huron storms and the other lakes are the suddenness and sometimes violence of the storms, and the sharpness of the waves. In the South Pacific the waves may be 30 feet high but they are far apart and roll. The Great Lakes waves are close together and have steep sides, and sometimes appear to spring up underneath the boat. A few years ago on one of the lakes an ore carrier broke up with a loss of all hands. These ore carriers are only exceeded in size by the great ocean tankers. So, for this and other reasons we wanted to get to Chicago and back into the river and canal system before the fall storms.

We did spend two extra days in Sarnia waiting for a storm to clear and then began our march up the U.S. shore of Huron. We hopped from refuge to refuge making 35 to 75 miles a day touching Sanilac, Harbor Beach, Tawas City, Thunder Bay and Rogers city. We had an occasional wind in which we could sail, but the "iron wind" (the sailor's affectionate name for their engines) drove us most of the way. We felt comfortable with our dependable Ford-Lehman 87 horsepower diesel. Our two previous boats had very light engines (18-20 hp) and a couple of times proved inadequate for our needs.

We had one exciting event as we were traveling from East Tawas to Thunder Bay. We were motoring along and had just passed Harrisville, when out of the radio came the call "Mayday! mayday! mayday! I'm on fire!" I waited about 20 seconds but heard no response from the Coast Guard.

I pressed the mike button and said, "Vessel calling mayday, what is your location?" This is, of course, most urgently needed, since a voice out of the radio tells you little. If the location is known, near-by vessels can respond.

There was no response. The Coast Guard then came on the air with the same query. No response. Then a boat came on the air saying that they were a sailboat and could see a column of smoke about 3 miles distant. The Coast Guard asked, "What is your location?"

The skipper gave his exact latitude and longitude from his loran and then reported that the column of smoke was bearing 147 degrees.

The Coast Guard thanked him and asked him to stand by. Then a voice came on the air and said, "This is the tug Molly Ann. I'm in Harrisville harbor and can be at the site in about 10 minutes."

The Coast Guard said, "Go ahead."

Tug: "I'm already under way."

Ten minutes passed with the coast guard organizing a nearby station to dispatch a vessel, conversations with local sheriffs, etc.

Then: "This is tug Molly Ann, I'm approaching the site, the boat has burned to the water line and the man is in the water. I'll have him aboard in a couple of minutes."

Coast guard: "Is he alive?"

Tug: "Yes, standby," after a pause, "He seems OK."

Coast Guard: "Can you put him on the radio?"

Tug: "No, he is pretty much in shock. Wait until I get some coffee in him."

We followed this drama for another half hour but it got buried in bureaucratese, such as where to land him, arranging for an ambulance and other matters involving which county, or township, or agency should do what.

Two things stood out from this event. First, the competence of the sailboat skipper who knew right where he was and who looked around the horizon, a habit you develop on watches at sea. Second, the tug boat captain who also knew where he was but who had the seamanship to plot the disaster's location and get underway quickly. To them that man owes his life.

Our loran (a device that uses radio waves to find your position) was on the fritz, but it's value to others had just been demonstrated. I had not been in a hurry to get it repaired since with the radar on board I didn't think it was necessary for our use. Its value to others had just been demonstrated. When we got to Mackinaw City, I ordered a new one from a catalogue and sent the faulty one off to the factory to be repaired. Maybe I too can save someone's life by knowing our own position instantly.

We had a great time once we got to Mackinaw City. The town was small, friendly and had a good modern marina. There are several good restaurants and a super market was a short distance away if we rode our folding bicycles. When we arrived at the marina we had barely secured our dock lines when a chap came strolling rapidly up with a cheerful, "Welcome to Mackinaw City. That burgee at your spreader earns you a free trip to the super market." He referred to our SSCA (Seven Seas Cruising Association) flag.

"My name is Larry Davis. Welcome to Mack City. Donna, My wife, and I spend our winters in the Bahamas on a sailboat, and have a small power-boat here. We are also members of the SSCA."

Larry and Donna made our stay in Mackinaw City very enjoyable.

As I said before, the Kellers are pretty lucky when it comes to festivals. On Labor Day each year, the Mackinaw

Bridge closes one of it's lanes and thousands of people walk across it. The bridge is affectionately called "Big Mack" and it is four miles across it. This bridge, spanning the Straits of Mackinac was completed fifteen years earlier and the cutting of the ribbon by the governor was followed by a walk across all four miles of the bridge. The governor and the public had so much fun they decided to do it every year.

We decided to join the 70,000 who made it this year. When 70,000 people descend on a village of 200 population (winter) there had to be some form of crowd control. Since this was to be the 15th annual "walk" they did have things pretty well worked out. You were bused across the bridge to St. Ignace where you got off and walked back. All of the school buses for miles around were pressed into service. The lines to board the busses were 3 to 4 abreast and snaked back and forth in a huge open space controlled by temporary fencing. It took us only one half hour to get up to the bus boarding area. When I looked back the lines were still just as full as when we started.

It was incredible that so many people would descend on this small town for such a worthless purpose, and they have been doing it for 15 years! One old codger proudly displayed his vest which contained his collection of 15 patches, one for each year. He was there, he said, when the Governor opened the bridge 15 years ago and walked across with him. He had actually heard him say, "We had so much fun we ought to do this every year." The old codger hadn't missed a walk since them, by golly!

When Ted and Liz arrived we took off for the more isolated areas of the North Channel. We dropped anchor in isolated bays and watched deer feed on the shore. We searched for moose and bear, which we were told could be seen, without success. We hiked through park-like woods on uninhabited islands and explored their shores by dinghy. We sailed the boat many times, which was a treat for me. To get there, it seems, we had been in too much of a hurry to hoist the sails and only do two or three knots when five to six were available from our engine. Up there in that pristine wilderness if we only did two or three knots, so what? We didn't have to get any where. Ted was an experienced sailor so one day we broke out the spinnaker and had a glorious sail for several miles until the wind picked up and we began to be over powered.

We docked at the tiny Canadian town of Meldrum. It consists of a church, a general store-post office, and, I think, a gas pump. There are people about from time to time but they live "over there about two miles" and for the most part are "summer people" who come from Toronto. The Indians and a few local non-Indians are the permanent inhabitants of the Island. It would be a wonderful place to live if you wanted to get away from it all. Did I mention it was on one of the larger islands?

Next to Meldrum is Vidal Bay. We dropped the hook in Vidal and settled in for two or three days of relaxation. We might have done more exploring in other bays and islands, but the winds were continuing strong and open transits to other places would have been, well, challenging. And, besides, this was an idyllic place.

The first thing we did was explore the shores. At the entrance to a small creek we observed several large salmon trying to swim up the creek. The water was too shallow at the entrance but they never gave up trying. They would wriggle up in the shallows until their backs were exposed and they could go no farther. They would then return to deeper water. Ten or twenty minutes later they (or others) would try again. We saw 15 or 20 fish and they were large — 10 to 30 pounds. Our excitement mounted!

We returned to Elizabeth M, hoisted the anchor and motored over to the store at Meldrum Bay. There we purchased some fishing tackle, Canadian licenses, and, optimistically, some lemons to put on the fresh salmon while it was barbecuing. By the way, can you imagine two people who live on the water and don't have proper fishing tackle? We did have a deep-sea rod and reel that we used on oceans, but nothing for this kind of fishing. The store owner confirmed that yes, he had heard that the salmon were in Vidal Bay, and suggested that we troll across the deeper center of the bay. He said that the fish commission had stocked that small stream with fingerlings about four years ago and he was happy that they had come back.

Happily we returned to Vidal Bay, dropped the anchor again, unshipped the dinghy, and suggested that the ladies warm up the frying pan. Well, we trolled all afternoon — no luck. We trolled in the morning — no luck. We cast from the shore. Our lures went right by their noses and they ignored them. We saw zip staring us in the face. Those darn fish were so intent on getting up that creek that they had no time to feed. Or so we thought. All fishermen need positive re-enforcement, and so Ted and I aired a number of perfectly logical theories.

We had planned to go to Meldrum in the afternoon and then leave for a leisurely trip back to Mackinaw City. After lunch, Ted and I decided to make a few more passes across the bay before we hoisted the anchor. Emily asked if she could go with us. Sure, we said. Again Ted and I zeroed out and reached the point of "one more pass and then we will go home." Emily said, "May I have one of the poles and try my luck?"

"Of course," I replied.

She scrounged in the tackle box and brought out a bass lure that she had tossed into our purchases at the store.

"Dear," I said, patiently, "That is not the proper lure for salmon. The man at the store recommended these other ones."

"Do you mind terribly if I use it anyhow?" she asked.

Being a husband, I replied, indulgently, "Of course not, go ahead, use it."

Of course, by now you can suspect what happened about half way across the bay. It took us about 10 minutes to land it. In the process we broke the net and Ted had to grab it and heroically bring it aboard by hand. We had grilled salmon that night, although I ate crow.

Another highlight was our visit to Mackinac Island, the home of the world renowned Grand Hotel. It has not changed from its gracious symbol of leisurely elegance. The island has no cars, not even golf carts. The only motor driven vehicles are the fire truck and an ambulance. Horses provide the motive power for cabs, which are painted yellow, and for tour buses, carriages, and freight. A number of street sweepers keep the streets tidy. Ted, being somewhat of a clown, grabbed a shovel from one of the sweepers and shoveled several loads into the wheelbarrow while I happily clicked my camera. For our tour of the island we rented a limousine with a fringe on top and a couple of nags called Rose and Bess.

The island was originally French, but John Jacob

Astor established a fur trading company there and the home of his agent still stands. There are many other historic buildings there including those of the Fort Mackinac. Imagine the strategic value of this fort where three of the great lakes are joined together. We lunched on a veranda that was 300 years old, and watched a cannon firing and a fife and drummer performance.

Emily, who had decided to learn the penny whistle, had a long musical conversation with the fifer.

Ted, back on his farm in New Hampshire, is the proud owner of a cannon not unlike that which the pseudo-soldiers were firing. He discussed technicalities with the cannoneers. I, a novice, had little to say because the only time I fired Ted's cannon, the axle on the carriage broke. The Youngs are a part of the colorful New Hampshire people and when Senator Bob Dole and his wife Elizabeth visited that area a couple of years ago, the senator declined to fire Ted's cannon, so his wife eagerly volunteered. Elizabeth Dole for President!

It is also a story told often that the neighbors complained to the sheriff about the loud reports from Ted's cannon. The sheriff came around and after seeing the cannon asked, "Can I fire it?"

We returned to Mackinaw City and said good-bye to these two fun people and made plans to meet them again in a year or so when we would be back in tropical waters.

## 10

## *LAKE MICHIGAN, CHICAGO BARGE AND SANITARY CANAL, ILLINOIS RIVER, ST. LOUIS.*

In Mackinaw City, as we were poised for the run down Lake Michigan to Chicago, we were visited by some rather foul weather which delayed our leaving. The local citizens had assured us that Indian summer was just around the corner and that we would have several weeks of fine weather. We, therefore, started out on a beautiful day for Beaver Island, which was about halfway across the upper end of Lake Michigan. The guide book had described the bay on Beaver Island as having good "holding," an important factor when you wake up in the night with a strong breeze blowing. In poor holding your anchor can, and usually does, drag. This means you must post an anchor watch and expect to lose some sleep.

The day remained sunny but after we had gone beyond the lee of the peninsula I was a little apprehensive about the waves but decided they were manageable. As we turned south to go through a cut in a rocky reef we were heading directly into the wind and Lizzie M started to kick up her heels — literally. As we entered the cut Lizzie dove into a trough and scooped a couple of tons of water over her foredeck. "Emily," I said, "The next flat place we will turn around and head back."

"Thank goodness," she said, "I just don't like this. It can't be Indian Summer yet. Maybe tomorrow."

Three days later a calm day was forecast, but as we looked out of the marina we saw solid fog. The fog was predicted to lift by 10:00 so we left the harbor about 9:00 navigating by radar. The ferries to Mackinac Island were leaving and arriving and a couple of them passed us in the fog. The bridge "Big Mack" stood out as a long straight line on the radar scope. I was having a great time, but I think Emily was just nervous.

I had operated radar during WWII and knew how to identify the patterns on the scope. This was the first time I had ever navigated in the fog. Visibility was about 20 feet but I knew where everything was. Emily didn't. I suppose this is a "guy thing." Radar was invented so that ships could continue on their way in fog.

As we passed under the center of the bridge the fog began to thin. A blip on the radar screen ahead turned out to be a motor yacht. I called him on the radio to check if our radar target was working. This is a device you attach to a high spot on the boat. It makes your boat look about the size of a naval vessel. He assured me that we had a strong echo. This was a relief. The last time I had asked anyone this question was in the Irish Sea. We were talking to a freighter out of Liverpool, and he responded, "Just a minute, I'll have to turn my radar on." So much for the safety value of the device.

This time we slid easily through the pass in the reef and turned right toward Beaver Island. It loomed on the horizon as we enjoyed the day, the sun and the fresh air. I became puzzled as the island seemed to shrink as we approached it. Now that's not normal — all the other islands grow as you get closer. We finally decided that a fog bank was engulfing the island, but the north end was still clear. We hurried to get there before we were socked in.

No such luck. As we came to within a mile the fog closed in, and once again we turned to radar. The chart showed two buoys at the entrance, and the entrance was wide, so we again navigated by radar. Again, I was on a high. The two buoys showed up clearly on the scope so I approached them at about 2 knots favoring the southern one. Soon, right on target it loomed out of the fog. We corrected course and continued. Within minutes we had burst out of the fog and there, in sparkling sunshine, was our harbor! This wisp of dense fog had curled around and across our path. A few minutes later I glanced back, and the fog had disappeared. Ah! the fickleness of nature.

Beaver Island would have been a marvelous place to spend a few days and relax, but the weather patterns were making us nervous, and the island is in the middle of the lake. The next morning we got an early start for Manistique on the north west coast. The name reminded us how strong the French influence is throughout the Great Lakes area.

Our next stop was down the west coast to a neat little harbor called Detroit Harbor on Detroit Island. It is one of the several islands and reefs that guard Green Bay from Lake Michigan proper. This was a long day in that we had covered nearly sixty miles.

A word here perhaps about our traveling habits. We consider a six hour day as a "normal." This translates at six knots to thirty six nautical miles. When we have a long distance to travel we start early, say 7:00 A.M. and have breakfast while traveling. We also will arrive as late as 6:00 P.M. For some time we had been amazed at how easily we had covered our fifty mile days, arriving at 2:30 in the afternoon. We attributed this to currents, wind, a false knotmeter or what ever seemed plausible at the time.

The truth finally dawned on us. The inland charts for the U. S. were all measured in statute miles. Our knotmeter read in nautical miles. A nautical mile is 6080 feet, while a statute mile is 5280. When we were traveling at six knots, our normal speed, we were actually doing almost seven miles per hour.

So now we knew why our "six hour" days were turning into "five hour" days.

Next we moved down the west coast of Lake Michigan to Baily's Harbor, a nice anchorage, and then Sturgeon Bay. There we were pinned down for four days by nasty weather outside on the big lake. We were afraid that Indian summer was not going to arrive until next June. Sturgeon Bay has lots of boats and several boat yards and might have been a good place to rest a little, but we really wanted to be out of the Great Lakes at this time of year. We had heard too many horror stories of what storms do to their surface.

On the fourth day the wind died, so we decided to run down about twenty miles to Manitowoc. We stayed there for several days, partly due to the weather (one day there was a light snow on the deck) but also due to the fact that we met some wonderful people there. After three days we did try to head south but the violence of the waves discouraged us and we returned to our slip in Manitowoc. On that day we seriously considered leaving our boat in Manitowoc for the winter.

In spite of the above recitation of doom, we had a wonderful time in Manitowoc. On the day we arrived at Manitowoc's fine, new, marina, we were approached by several people who were curious about our boat, since not many world cruisers call there and certainly not many from Portland, Oregon. Among the curious were Frank and Eva Kraler. They saw to it that we did not feel lonely in their town.

The town of Manitowoc is neat and well maintained, in spite of the periodicity of its buildings. Its new waterfront development includes a marine museum of impressive stature. One of the exhibits is a huge submarine moored just outside the museum in the river. A large number of submarines had been built in Manitowoc during WWII. They were placed on barges that resembled floating dry docks and floated down the Illinois and Mississippi on much the same track as we planned to take. The sub moored there was built there, had seen service in the war, retired afterward and then given to the city as a memorial.

Another endearing feature of the town was the second confectionery of our trip. This one was almost a duplicate of the one in Ainsworth, Nebraska, complete with plywood booths and paper flowers entwined around a wooden lattice. There in Manitowac, I revisited my childhood with a strawberry ice cream soda. Frank and Eva took us there for lunch intending to surprise us with a trip back in time but for me it was just a return to the happy days of youth.

We followed that with a trip through the country and a brief walk over hill and dale. The landscape consisted of rolling hills and stands of trees held apart by large grassy expanses. In some cows contentedly munched the rich grass and occasionally we would skirt a small lake. It was pretty obvious why Wisconsin is considered the "Dairy State." The trees were beginning to don their fall colors, so it was a particularly pleasant walk.

Daily we climbed the stairs of the marina office and from the balcony gazed out with our binoculars in a vain hope for a calm lake and little wind. Rain pelted us. Water froze on the deck at night. We negotiated with the marina manager for possible storage space on land for Elizabeth M. A huge "laker" (you have to see one of these behemoths to appreciate their size) anchored off shore with two tugs standing by to avoid being blown aground. Obviously the Indian summer had opted for winter.

A day arrived with no wind, the laker had come on in to port, and, although there was ice on the deck, we decided to make a run for Port Washington, about 30 miles south. A quick telephone goodby to Frank and Eva, and we were off!

The sea was flat so we made good time. I was able to hoist my down wind sails for the first time in months. From Port Washington another dash down to Racine, reluctantly bypassing Milwaukee, and then the next day stopping at Waukegan. Although we took a short walk into the city we saw no sign of Jack Benny. There was one statue whose name was thoughtfully obscured — but it didn't look like Benny or Rochester.

The next day gale-force winds were forecast, so we decided not to make the jump down to Chicago — another 40 miles. The weatherman was wrong, and as the day wore on we lamented our decision. But when it comes to weather we always err on the side of caution, having paid our dues in that department. Our record for seven years is eight serious storms of which three were hurricanes.

The towers of Chicago beckoned us in the distance. We answered the call early the next morning, wanting to make port quickly for two reasons. The first was to have the masts taken down again as the journey down the Chicago Barge Canal included some rather low bridges and there were some in the Illinois River. The second reason was that anchoring in Chicago's outer harbor was chancy. Just two weeks earlier a storm had destroyed some boats anchored there. We phoned ahead to the marina which could lower our masts and hoped to get them down quickly and move into the canal that evening.

Nothing ever works out as you have planned, but a benevolent weather god smiled at us and we were able to spend a quiet night in the outer harbor. Oh, the masts got down, all right, but no place in the canal for miles could take us, even for a night and we did want to spend a few days in Chicago — but not in the outer harbor. Finally, late in the evening, a marina listed in the guide said that we could tie up there the next day on their outer pier for several days.

The next day was bright and sunny (had the Indian

Summer finally arrived?) and the Sears and Hancock Towers and the other beautiful buildings scintillated in the clear fresh air. Our Mecca! Our cloud castle floating in the sky! At this point I feel compelled to remind you that we had literally fought our way down the west shore of Lake Michigan. We knew that once we got to Chicago storms would no longer be much of a problem. We would not have to huddle in harbors while the storms whipped the lake to a fury outside the sea walls. In the rivers and canals we could travel at our convenience and stop pretty much as we wished. And this is why Chicago shone like a fairy castle before us. It is also a very beautiful city.

The barge canal flows — figuratively, not literally, as there is no current — through the center of the city. We timidly thrust our bow into the canal and prepared to be overwhelmed by these huge towers of commerce that shown in the morning sun. Overwhelmed we were. I have been in most of the big cities of the world, and tall buildings don't impress me. But, standing on the after deck and gazing up 50 or 60 stories on either side to a narrow patch of blue sky would be a new experience to any boat owner who has not been on the Chicago Barge Canal.

Above of us on the bridges people scurried to their offices carrying their brief cases. Cars, busses and trains crossed the canal, and two retired gray-haired adventurers slowly moved through their midst. Those who know Chicago know that many low bridges span the canal. All of them open — but I doubt that we could have gotten even one of them to open. Our marina was a short distance beyond the Sears Tower. We were soon tied up and registered. The Marina was a ground level part of a large apartment complex. In addition to the marina there was a small, but complete, grocery store and The National Television Museum. One day, a Saturday, we were working outside on the boat and Emily said, "Look at all those sailboats. They are just circling around between those two bridges."

I looked up to see a large number of sailboats trapped by their masts between two bridges and nothing happening. Soon the bridge on our side opened and they all moved through and circled between the next two bridges. The next bridge opened and the whole flock of perhaps thirty boats motored slowly by and on down the canal. We eventually got the whole story. These boats had been moored outside in the harbor or at other marinas for the summer. By agreement among the Yacht clubs and the city, one weekend is scheduled for them to come in through the city. The city then puts on an extra bridge tender (I think there are only two for about 22 bridges.) and the flotilla then goes through, a bridge at a time. The bridge tender must travel from bridge to bridge in order to operate them. Seems to work!

We did the tourist bit both of us revisiting the Museum of Science and Industry. We visited the Chicago Art Institute for a pleasant afternoon. And we did a bit of downtown strolling during which I got talked into a new lap top computer with the latest innovation, a hard drive.

When we entered the outer harbor we slowly circled the Navy Pier where I had trained for six months to become an ETM (Electronic Technicians Mate) during WWII. I pointed it out to Emily: there is about where my bunk was, there is where the mess was and there, out at the end, is where our graduation was held.

I have many fond memories of Chicago from that World War II experience. It was known as possibly the best liberty town in the U. S. The USO could, and would, supply you with almost any entertainment: tickets to concerts, free passes to movies, free meals at churches and other organizations. The USO hostesses even knew which churches had the prettiest volunteer servers. Service men and women truly were guests of that city.

Until we got to the Illinois River, there was not much to be said for the Chicago Sanitary and Barge Canal. It went in pretty much a straight line through depressing industrial areas. Except for a couple of anxious moments dodging barges, one which completely blocked all traffic, we spent the day cautiously threading our way through the area. In this respect, although at this point, we had traveled several thousand of miles in canals, we had encountered little commercial traffic. In France, we passed perhaps ten peniches, the motorized barges. In the ICW perhaps a half-dozen and in the Erie all we saw were a few canal work barges and none were moving — just moored.

The Illinois, on the other hand, has much commercial activity. We passed many barges, loaded and unloaded, and usually in clusters. The largest cluster was 15 barges lashed together and pushed by one tug, of course. Frequently we passed grain elevators in the process of dumping the fall's harvest of corn, wheat or other grains into the holds of the barges. We saw barges loaded to the water line with coal in front of power plants and others with sand for the cement canyons of the cities. It soon became apparent to us that having a river or canal pretty much to ourselves was a thing of the past. We had to get into the habit of approaching blind areas cautiously and to keep the radio on at all times. Tugs talk to each other, and, they anticipate each other's needs and problems. Pleasure boats are pretty much ignored so you can cut the odds against you by being alert and showing a little intelligence and consideration. Contrary to what you might think, they do not want to run you down. They will tell you if they need "the whole river" to make a turn. But, of course, you have to let them know that you are there by announcing your approach to a blind corner if you know that tugs are in the area.

Our conception of Illinois is that it is heavily wooded because most of the river is heavily wooded. The reason for this is that it is lined with marshes which only the shallowest of skiffs can explore. Great for ducks! Above Peoria the river widened out into a lake which kicked up some waves in a strong breeze as we crossed it. The channel was well marked and went straight across the lake, but it was a little disconcerting to see duck blinds less than 30 yards from the channel.

Peoria seemed to be a prosperous little city but we didn't stop for a visit. There had been frost on our deck that morning. We pulled into the Illinois Valley Yacht Club for the night and planned to leave early in the morning. We now had an objective — St. Louis. We had phoned ahead to the Harbor Pointe Marina in West Alton, Illinois and they could handle us for the winter. The next day we made 82 miles! I guess it was a record. We had spent the last six winters in the tropics or in warm countries and we just weren't prepared to handle frost and freezing. We wanted to be settled into a berth and all arrangements made before the winter snows began.

The rest of the Illinois was uneventful with one exception. We tried to pass a barge on his starboard, or right, side and nearly got squeezed into the bank. I called him on the radio. He acknowledged, and then I attempted a couple more comments which were acknowledged by an unintelligible remark. I couldn't understand why he had responded in such a way. I was already halfway up his tow.

Then around the bend, without his having signaled came another 3x5 tow (three barges wide and five long). Two thick tows approaching each other at high speed at a bend in a narrow channel is not conducive to casual conversation — nor does the tug captain give a damn about you or where you are when he is in a situation like that. Being so far advanced in the passing I pushed the throttle to the max and Lizzie M labored slowly, much too slowly, past the barges and finally was in the clear. Both Emily and I then resumed breathing.

The only other excitement was just before we burst out on to the Mississippi. We saw six snow white pelicans standing on a log where a small slough entered the river. We told a fellow this later here in the marina and he refused to believe us. They were heron or egrets, he said. Well, Emily and I know pelicans. And we have seen a lot of white herons and egrets. We have lived with the sea for six years and seen pelicans all over the world, including white ones! So there!

Our excitement grew as we approached the Mississippi I was afraid that I would be disappointed when we finally arrived — but I was not. The Illinois widened and deepened and there were several navigable side channels and more islands. Soon the river widened a little and two islands lay ahead. Between the two islands we could look out on a large expanse of water and ahead lay a huge bluff. We had arrived!

As we passed the last island the mighty Mississippi lay before! The opposite shore was distant and the water was deeper and stretched out almost endlessly before us. A huge 3x6 tow was approaching — but, who cared? The channel was now a half mile wide! A paddle wheel riverboat passed us (full of tourists I think). If I needed more assurance that we were actually on the father of waters, there it was. They were actually using their paddles for propulsion! A gang plank hung off the bow, just as in the old prints. Incidentally, a stern wheeler creates one helluva wake. Lizzie bobbed and rolled as violently as on a stormy ocean.

All the riverboats we had seen before were excursion boats with lots of gingerbread driven by propellers with fake paddle wheels and fake stacks. This boat's stack was real but I don't think that the smoke coming out of it was from cut wood.

We did not need Mark Twain's advice in "Life on the Mississippi," which I had studiously read. The river is completely buoyed, and one need only stay between the buoys to avoid the sandbars which gave pilot Sam Clemens so much trouble.

We found the Marina (Harbor Pointe) in West Alton, Ill. about 13 miles below where we had entered the Miss. It is a beautiful, new marina and the only one with depth enough to handle our six foot draft. It had been planted a few years ago with gum and maple trees which were already approaching full fall brilliance. The personnel were all pleasant and competent and the facilities new and adequate. We felt that we were leaving Elizabeth M in good hands. She was soon up on the hard and tucked snugly under a tarp.

There she spent the winter.

## 11

## *MISSISSIPPI RIVER, OHIO RIVER, TENNESSEE RIVER*

We returned to Elizabeth M in mid-March, and as requested, Lizzie had been put in the water at the Marina and was waiting for us near the fuel dock. Happily we boarded her, aired her out and settled in. The next day I went to the yard foreman and asked if we could put up Lizzie's masts as we were anxious to get out on the river and go adventuring. He said that he hoped so, but since he had put Lizzie in the water the river had gone down a couple of feet, and he didn't think we could get to the crane. If the river should rise in the next day or two we could do it; otherwise we would have to just wait.

Well — tides we have dealt with all over the world. Rivers were new to us, and there didn't seem to be much we could do but wait. So we did!

There was a stick on the bank a few inches above the water line near our boat. We watched it daily, and the water appeared only to recede from the stick, instead of rising. We had hoped to be at least in the Ohio River in two weeks since we were planning a trip to Europe to meet friends on April 1. We rented a car and saw a lot more of St. Louis, more than we wanted to see, including dead fish.

Dead fish? Yes, the marina was full of them. When we arrived we asked the yard superintendent about them. The Marina freezes each winter, and this winter had been particularly severe. The fish froze and died, he said, and when the ice thawed they just floated up to the surface. This made us even happier that we had had Elizabeth M hauled out on to land and winterized. To winterize you must flush out all water and replace it, in the engine especially, with antifreeze. We had covered Lizzie with a tarp, so we assumed she had had a restful winter.

As the middle of the second week approached we became desperate to "do something." Not only could we not move over to the crane area but now we could not even move our boat over to the fuel dock thirty or forty feet away. We were mired in the mud. We decided to call a crane out from the city and at least put the mast up so that when we returned from Europe we could start right out — assuming that the river would have risen by then!

The crane arrived but could not do the job because a tree interfered with his boom. But if we could just move about thirty feet forward he could do it. We turned on the engine and tried, with full power, to inch forward. We never moved a centimeter. The crane operator had an idea. If we used our power and some of his maybe we could move the boat.

He attached his lifting line to our bow and lifting the bow up with us on full power we literally plowed forward enough for his purpose! Of course, we settled down into the mud again, but we soon had the masts up and were ready to leave when we returned in about a month — providing the river had risen!

The river had risen, our masts were up and after shopping for a few fresh foods, on June 1, we poked Elizabeth M's bow out into the broad river before us. It had been some time since I had been at the wheel of Lizzie and a feeling of exultation and excitement over the adventures that lay before us welled up in me. Two things were immediately obvious. The current was much faster than we had imagined, and the water was full of snags and driftwood.

The first tow (a raft of barges) that we encountered was humongous. The largest tow we saw on the Mississippi was a 6x10, that is six barges wide by ten barges long all creating an area the size of a football field. Someone, I don't remember who, claimed they had seen one 9x8.

These large masses are pushed by a tug that is mostly engine. The helmsmen sits in a tower that rises twenty to thirty feet in the air so that he has a clear view of the river and can anticipate moves that must be taken. It takes them a mile or two to stop, and turns must be anticipated hundreds of yards in advance. There is a "dead spot" just ahead of the barges that the pilot cannot see and into which a small boat could disappear (forever) without the pilot knowing it. Fortunately tows this large are only found on the Mississippi. We, of course, and all other surviving small boaters on the Mississippi, treat them with respect and give them all the river that they need.

As we approached the first bridge just below the marina both Emily and I became nervous. Our judgement had been so dulled by our long absence from the boat that Emily said, "I don't think we can make it under that bridge."

"I'm sure we can," I replied without much conviction, "But maybe we had better take it easy going under it. This current is so strong though that we couldn't stop quickly enough as we are swept under it."

"What can we do?" Emily asked.

"Well, lets back under it."

"How will that help?"

"If we are going down stream with a three knot current and are traveling up stream at the rate of two and a half knots; we should just barely creep under the bridge — Right?"

"Absolutely brilliant!" answered my greatest fan.

My plan worked but fell a little flat when we cleared the bridge by about 30 feet.

We negotiated our first lock on the Miss. not long after leaving the marina, and then went by downtown St. Louis. This was an impressive sight, dominated, of course by the giant golden arch over the waterfront. The quay was lined with excursion boats, all but one built to resemble the paddle wheel steamers of the a romantic era of the past. The one boat not built to resemble gaudy sternwheelers was obscenely constructed of shiny stainless steel and looked like a rocket ship.

We were now in Mark Twain's country and we eagerly recalled that romantic era when the sternwheel steamer was king of the river. Their greatest importance was not in the well dressed passengers and gamblers that booked passage. The high tonnage of cargo that they brought to the southern market and the manufactured goods that they brought back made many a river captain wealthy.

I would like to say that our trip down the Miss. to the Ohio was exciting, but it was really rather dull. The river is huge, the shoreline a monotonous strip of trees, there are few marinas or places to stop, and only an occasional town breaks the sameness. The Ohio River was about 180 miles from St. Louis and there we would leave the father of waters and explore America's heartland via some of its tributaries.

The first night we spent at a small moorage on the shore, and the current flowing past our boat was about 3 knots. We arrived there early in the day and the reason we had stopped, although it was only 30 miles down the river, was because it was the only marina between St. Louis and the Ohio. We had located an anchorage at mile 78 (measured from the Ohio upstream — St. Louis was at about mile 190), but it was too far to be reached in one day, or so we thought, so we took the easy way out and only knocked off 30 miles the first day.

The next day we raced on down the river, passing large tows, some that were five or six barges wide and nine or ten long. I said "raced" because at the end of the day when we anchored behind the island as planned, I calculated that we had traveled at a speed of eleven (statute) miles per hour while our knot meter was kept at about six knots (nautical miles per hour). That current was impressive! Behind the island the current was still substantial, but much less than in the river. We worried a little about our anchor holding, but I remembered that sand is just about the best "holding" ground that you can have. Our anchor line was stretched, but I knew was more than adequate to hold the boat. We slept soundly after we had dozed off to the sleepy twittering of the birds in the trees on the island.

The next day, except for a sudden deepening of the water from 16 feet to 140 feet, there were no thrills on the river. The only reason that was a thrill is because the man (or woman — Emily is an excellent helmsperson) glances at the depthsounder frequently and it is startling to glance down and see that the reading has jumped to 80 ft. and then to 100 feet as you watch. You look around to see what is happening because of this phenomenon. A slight boil on the surface and a couple of stray currents is about all.

However, the highlight of the day occurred when we were just short of the island at the junction of the two rivers where we had planned to spend the night. We had traveled 75 miles, it was late, and we were anxious to get the hook down and relax. Just before the island we passed three people in a small boat. The father had the cover off of the motor and the wife and daughter were watching him rather dejectedly. We slowed down.

"Do you need help?" Emily called.

"Our motor won't run," said the woman.

"Do you have any oars?" Emily asked.

"Just this," The man held up a small piece of board.

"Then you need help," I said. We turned upriver, came alongside and Emily tossed them one of our mooring lines. It turned out that they had to go about a half a mile down the Miss, then about two miles up the Ohio. Our anchoring spot was about 100 yards down the river. It was 6:00 P.M. The round trip would take about an hour and a half. My stomach was complaining.

But, the code of the sea is strong. You must render assistance to vessels in distress.

Proceeding slowly, we traveled the distance and released them at the boat ramp just below Cairo. During the interminably long trip (I apologize for the selfish nature of that adjective) we became quite well acquainted, since they were just a few feet from our stern. We were invited to their home for dinner, and it was difficult to turn them down. We were tired after a long day (80 miles) and anxious to get the anchor down and relax.

A half hour later with the anchor down, I was relaxing on the after-deck listening to the evening concert of the birds and to the sounds of Emily's preparation for dinner coming up from the galley. I pondered two things as I sipped my aperitif. Why does it make you feel so good and content when you have really helped someone in trouble — to the point that you totally forgot why it was so important to stick strictly to your planned schedule? Secondly; Why wasn't I hungry anymore?

The Ohio is certainly wide and deep. It is said by the locals, in Ohio and Illinois that is, that the Mississippi River really empties into the Ohio, instead of the opposite. The current was slight, and there was almost no floating debris. This was a blessing since we were traveling upriver. We only had 50 miles to go before we would reach the Tennessee and our objective, a marina just past the confluence of the two rivers. Just as we reached Paducah, a fearsome thunderstorm struck. We quickly scrubbed our plan to go a short distance up the Tennessee to the marina. I elected to tie up to a barge that appeared to have been made for boats to tie up while visiting the motel on the shore.

Emily shouted over the roar of the storm, "Are you sure that it is OK for us to tie up there?"

"Lady," I replied, "I don't give a damn! This is an emergency and I care more about us and our boat than I do about whether they want us to tie there, or not. Besides, we might put a little drama into the day of those fat cats sitting there in the lounge and watching that sailboat out there struggling in the storm."

"I like your attitude," she said.

So, I brought Lizzie alongside and that brave little slip of a woman jumped onto the barge and secured our lines. An hour later the storm subsided, but we decided to stay the night. Nobody even came near us.

The first dam we encountered on the Tennessee river was the Kentucky dam. For those of you who are not familiar with this river-lake system, it was one of President Franklin Delano Roosevelt's dreams to dam all the rivers in the country that were suitable for the generation of hydro power. The country then was to be divided in to power "Authorities" that would sell this cheap power wholesale to the utilities in the area. Portions of the construction expense would be charged to recreation and commercial transportation. The Tennessee and our own Columbia River in the Pacific Northwest are the only areas to be developed in this manner.

The nation's insatiable demand for power has long exceeded the ability of these hydro dams, both public and private. The heavy commercial traffic, although substantial, has never reached the proportions that were dreamed. The recreational use, however, has exploded, and the majority of the traffic locking up or down is recreational and not commercial. On a weekend the lakes formed by these dams swarm with bass fisherman and an occasional world cruiser.

There are also many pontoon boats that consist of two floats supporting a bridge deck which may be open with an assortment of arrangements and fittings under a sometimes tasseled canopy. Some are totally enclosed houseboats designed for gracious living during the family's two week vacation. These craft are all shallow draft, so that you can explore coves and inlets and not be confined to the commercial channel, such as we were. Incidentally, these craft are for hire on many of the lakes. There are also more elaborate craft for hire with luxurious interiors that are not pontoon craft but still shallow draft.

The only negative aspect of these dams are the barrier they cause to the anadromous fish. On the Columbia River where the salmon fishery is a huge cash crop, this is important. The problem of getting the mature fish up the dams and the fingerlings down has never been satisfactorily solved. Regardless of the controversial aspects, these lakes formed by the great dams, certainly do provide a very positive recreational factor to a region.

The locks are huge. I would say that we have been through several hundred locks in our travels. On the Rhone river in France we ran into some pretty big ones of about 30 meters, nearly 100 feet. These on the Tennessee were of equal lift, the greatest lift being 100 feet, and the least that we encountered being 45 feet. The awesomeness of the locks is not so much in the lift as in the fact that you motor into a huge cavern, perhaps 150 ft by 600, feet and when the gates close behind you, you are in a huge deep square hole. The water swirls in, and you slowly rise to the next level.

Again, we were distressed, as on the Erie Canal, by the lack of suitable mooring for recreational boats. We tied to large floating bollards, which are moorings recessed into the walls. They float up as the water level rises and are placed about every 150 feet in the wall — a proper spacing for barges. A thirty-eight foot boat, however, has only one point to tie to and this is not a good way to tie. When the water surges in you are buffeted about. FDR was a yachtsmen, but he never envisioned that the "masses" would own boats and swarm over these areas. "Yachting" was for gentlemen who didn't have to ask how much it cost.

The name of the first dam, lock, and lake was Kentucky. Just above Kentucky dam we crossed over to the opposite side of the lake where the charts showed a state park and marina. We had heard that the parks in this lake-dam system were very nice but were not prepared for the beautiful facility that we found. The marina was new and modern. There was a boat launching ramp for the bass fisherman and a beautifully landscaped area for picnicking. Some of these parks have motels and first rate restaurants as a part of the facility. That, combined with numerous coves and inlets available for quiet anchorages, promised a summer of delightful cruising.

To travel up and down this great river-lake system is to be treated to one of the world's finest cruising experiences. You would think that we would have spent most of our time in Tennessee, but the river curves southward into Alabama before swooping back up into Tennessee. We have gone as far up the river as Chattanooga where we were blocked from going farther by a two week lock repair. We could have gone as far as Knoxville otherwise.

We did go up to Chattanooga on Lizzie, just to say

that we had been there, and returned to Hales Bar Marina about 10 miles down the river from Chattanooga. There are marinas in Chattanooga, but none of them would accommodate our 6-foot draft. Tennessee (and northern Alabama) is semi-mountainous and heavily forested. Imagine that you are traveling up the river through this kind of area. Your lake turns into a river for a few miles. Then as you round a bend you are greeted by a huge dam. You enter the lock, are raised from 50 to 100 feet and motor out into another wide lake, just as beautiful as the last. On Kentucky lake we stopped at Cuba Landing Marina which is near a point where I-40 crosses a narrow part of the lake and leads north into Nashville. We planned to meet our friend Betty Parker from Portland. We obtained a ride into the city to a motel from the marina owner. We took a bus tour of the city and saw all of the important places in this Capital of Country Music. We saw the multitude of recording studios, the Original Grand Ole Opry house, the estates of the many who have made fortunes from music, etc. That night we had dinner at a music house, with a headliner whom I didn't know, but then, I'm not a devotee.

The next day Betty arrived. We rented a car and knocked around Nashville and then returned to the boat via the marina taxi. For the next few days we just cruised, swam around the boat, ate great food as the two ladies tried to out-cook each other, and talked.

Betty's presence fills a need in Emily that I fill very poorly. She is utterly thrilled by a particular bird or flower. The Old Salt, appreciates such things but is not "utterly thrilled." Betty, on the other hand, is just as thrilled and enthusiastic as Emily. They would often take the dinghy and disappear for an hour or two, exploring an anchorage.

We anchored one night not far from the Shiloh Battlefield National Park, where one of the great and decisive battles of the Civil War was fought. The next morning we anchored off the battlefield and the two women went ashore with the folding bicycles and lunches. I stayed on the boat because our anchor did not catch on the first attempt we made, and I was not sure how well it had dug into the bottom on the second. Besides, we only had two bicycles. They returned tired and happy and full of recounts of their experiences.

These folding bicycles are usually standard equipment on cruiser's boats. They fold into a package about 8 by 18 by 24 inches and have small wheels, about 18 inches in diameter. There are several brands. The one we have folds the most compactly. Some have larger wheels, and many cruisers carry standard bikes that they disassemble and store below. Bicycles provide shoreside transportation to those places too far for a comfortable walk.

We stopped at Joe Wheeler Marina on the next lake up. Joe Wheeler Dam and Lake contain the highest lift on the Tennessee. Elizabeth M's mast did not reach very far up the wall of the lock.

This was where the captain over all the locks was located. He went strictly by the book. He wanted us to put on life jackets. I protested only mildly, and when he said that he would not let the water in until we did, we dug them out and donned them. We have been through hundreds of locks all over the world and this is the first, and only, time that this has been required of us.

We frequently are the only boat in the lock during the week. As I mentioned, there is not much commercial traffic, and when there is the lockmasters will lock them down first and then let us follow. If there is only one barge to the tow, and that is extremely rare, some lockmasters will let in pleasure boats at the same time. Most barge tows, here on the Tennessee, are two or four as the capacity of the locks is two wide and two long. When a larger tow comes up (or down) they must break up into the smaller units. We once spent two hours waiting for a tow to be broken up and put back together. The lockmaster promised to let us know when the lock would be free again — and he did.

We met some nice people at the Joe Wheeler Yacht Club, which was located at the marina. They invited us back to help them celebrate the Fourth with them. There would be races, prizes, a swap meet, a dinner and dance following. We made a mental note to return.

One person who came over to welcome us was Heidi. This attractive, dignified lady was a sales person for the Redstone Arsenal in Huntsville. When asked what she sold she said "Missiles." When we asked her husband, Clyde, what he did he said, "I play the bongos." Actually, we found out later, that he is a security specialist. These two interesting people own a sea-going sailboat and plan to join the cruising fraternity as soon as Heidi retires. They plied us with many questions about cruising life, but judging from the manner in which they had equipped their boat, they had done quite well so far.

Our next major stop after the Joe Wheeler Yacht Club was Huntsville, Alabama, where Betty rented a van and went to visit relatives for a week or two. Before she left we visited the Space Museum. Huntsville, as you may know, is the place where the German rocket scientists were brought following WWII. Germany, at that time was far ahead of the free world in rocket research and development.

Many military strategists believe that had the war lasted another year,the German rocket superiority would have changed its outcome. Both Russia and the United States offered these scientists incentives to join their causes. Those who joined the cause of the free world were brought to Huntsville.

The space museum contains most of the great space hardware of our history, including the lunar landing module and a scale mockup of a space shuttle. Definitely a must-see if you are anywhere in the neighborhood.

In the last six years we have celebrated the Fourth of July in many places in the world and in many ways, including completely overlooking it in foreign countries when no Americans were around. The most enjoyable celebration that will live longest in our memories may well be that which we celebrated with the Joe Wheeler Yacht Club. The co-sponsor was the Decatur Navy, which was based at Joe Wheeler marina on Joe Wheeler Lake above Joe Wheeler Dam. I asked, but could find no one who knew anything about Joe Wheeler! (Emily, true belle of the South that she is, was only mildly incensed by that last statement. Joe Wheeler, it seems, was a famous Southern General during the Civil War. I am happy to insert this explanation.)

So, on July 3rd we returned from Huntsville to the J. W. Marina, a short day trip, and found preparations well advanced. The most fascinating activity to me was the preparations for the "paper boat race." I had been urged to enter it and I now wish I had. I was completely mystified by the whole prospect. Build a boat out of paper? Ridiculous! The rules? Build a boat out of paper and sail it around a triangular course with your self in it. No other rules, except the fastest boat won the prize.

When we went over to inspect the construction area, I regretted that I had not entered the competition. With my heavy reading in naval architecture, my world class experience in boats and my great engineering skills, perhaps I could have done it. You were given a limited number of sheets of cardboard, two rather strong sticks, and all the duct tape, glue, and paint that you could use.

The designs varied from four square floats tied together with the two long sticks (designed, produced, and manned by four 10 to 12-year old girls who named their boat "The Four Babes") to a rather elaborate tug boat with pilot house and paddle wheel (designed produced and manned by a former tug captain). I think the winner was a sort of canoe. He won because he was a superb paddler using a kayak type paddle. He was not a great engineer, however, as his boat fell apart as it was being lifted out of the water at the end.

The four babes only made it about 20 feet away from the dock before their craft sank. They should have spent more time coordinating their paddling. They managed to rotate it fairly rapidly, but never achieved straight-line motion. The tug fell apart about halfway. Two women in a double kayak didn't waterproof (paint) sufficiently, but did finish the race by swimming the last 50 feet and pulling their soggy boat behind them. It was an hilarious event and I filed it away in my memory for some future time when our yacht club would have such an occasion.

There was a small boat sailing race, which I entered. There was virtually no wind and few of the boats finished the race. I got third by "sculling." This is the technique of moving the tiller back and forth rapidly so that the rudder acts as an oar.

It had been years since I had sailed a small class racing boat like this and I was disappointed that we had not had better sailing conditions. (Class racing is when all the boats are exactly alike.)

The banquet and dance on the evening of the 4th was threatened by thunderstorms that had been building up all day. There was a large shed, so we moved the tables in under it. Of course, it didn't rain! The debris of the paper boat construction had to be pushed aside and a space was cleared for dancing. The menu was worthy of the occasion, being green salad, a huge bucket of assorted steamed shellfish, watermelon, hot garlic bread and assorted cakes and pies.

While we sat around and groaned over our gluttony, the band tuned up. It consisted of an excellent keyboard artist from the Decatur Navy, a tub base, and Clyde, who lived up to his advanced billing, on the bongos. We danced and sang, and even had a "name that tune" contest. I won a prize, and astonished Emily, by identifying and singing the first line of one of the songs out of my generation. The song was "San Antone," and the prize was a small water pistol. During my youth the words and tune "Deep within my heart lies a melody, the song of old San Antone" were indelibly etched and recalled for this victorious moment.

The Decatur Navy put on a demonstration of superb piloting and boat handling. On the afternoon of the 5th we were all invited on board a group of the Navy's larger boats and treated to a sundown soiree of great appetizers and friendly hospitality. The six cruisers rafted up (tied together) out in the lake as we watched the sun disappear behind the trees.

We will always retain a warm friendly glow for the

people of the Huntsville-Decatur area.

As you proceed East up the Tennessee the surroundings change from more or less flat country to occasional hills and a few bluffs. The hills steepen and grow and the bluffs become more numerous until finally there is no doubt; you are now in the mountains. Ahead of you some rather prominent peaks rise up, but the river winds calmly around them. Every once and a while the depth sounder registered 50, 60, 70, even 108 feet — and the shores were only 50 feet away on either side of the boat!

One short stretch we approached rather hesitantly as we went on up the river toward Chattanooga was "Suck Shoals" and "The Suck." We had heard that the name came from the fact that barges in days of yore were sucked into the rapids at point labeled "Suck" and flung with complete loss of control on the shoal area below it. Most barges made it but about once a week, so the story goes, one was lost with its cargo. The barges were hauled up this rapid by cables on the shore, but were on their own on the down trip. When we passed through, it had been tamed partially by the damming of the river and partially by the more powerful engines of today. We were flung about only slightly and never felt threatened.

When you get close to Chattanooga, the air becomes hazy and it is evident why these are called the Great Smoky Mountains. We stood on top of the tallest mountain, Lookout mountain, near Chattanooga, which is a mere 2000 ft — not great by our Pacific Northwest standards. From our vantage point we could have seen seven states, if it had been clear. Several famous Civil War battles were fought on the sides of this mountain.

The nearest marina to Chattanooga that we could

find to accommodate our six-foot boat was at the previously mentioned Hales Bar Landing. These "landings" that we keep referring to are places where either a steamer once stopped, or where a ferry existed. We have paused at Ditto, Cuba, Hales Bar, and Kelley's Landings and passed many others. I am always curious about these names. Was there a Mr. or Mrs. Cuba? or Ditto? I suppose there was a person called Hale and Kelly, I can find a good reason for The Suck, and the Suck Shoals, but less than a half mile down stream from them there is a section of the river called Kettle, and another just beyond it called Skillet. One day I would enjoy researching some of these eccentric names.

We remained at Hales Bar Marina for several days, rented a car, and drove the approximately ten miles into Chattanooga each day. Those of our generation well remember the song that Glen Miller made famous — "Chattanooga ChooChoo." A Railroad Museum there contains the "original" Chattanooga Choochoo. I put original in quotes, because who would know the difference. Any-how, the mystery and the glory are in the words of the song and the superb rendition of the melody by the greatest of the great bands of our generation.

The museum contained many retired railroad cars that were restored to the grandness of the past when traveling by railroad was the usual thing and only the reckless traveled by plane. The grounds were being groomed and maintained by men all dressed alike and with a big "P" on their shirts. They were all working diligently and doing their jobs well — apparently unsupervised.

We chatted with one of them who said that he liked to do this because it "sure as hell beat sitting in a cell." He wasn't suppose to be talking to us but we looked like nice people, so he didn't mind taking a chance.

Another reason for visiting Chattanooga was Rock City. As a girl Emily had driven with her parents over a good portion of southeast United States; and all through this territory there were signs, frequently on the sides of barns, simply saying "Rock City." She never went there but had dreamed of going some day. Now, some fifty or more years later having arrived by boat up the Tennessee River, she was finally able to visit it. It is a rather unusual phenomenon. You can wander for several miles through natural tunnels and among boulders, much as you might wander down a winding city street.

This was well into July and the heat was becoming oppressive. Emily remembered this heat from her childhood and medical practice in a North Carolina town. She said that it would get worse, instead of better. She heaved a sigh of relief when I said, "Why don't we go home to our cool state of Oregon for a couple of months." She had thought that I wanted to keep sailing regardless of our discomfort. She was wrong. What fun is there in doing outdoor things when the only comfort you can get is in air-conditioned buildings? Besides, we are retired and have no reason to either prove our mettle, or to do things that are not fun.

Consequently, we moved Lizzie to a comfortable place, at Hales Bar Marina where she was under the watchful eyes of two new live-aboard friends, Avis and Bob Shoemaker. These two retired people had bought a rather spacious motor yacht (with lots of air conditioning) and moved aboard with no particular intentions of going cruising.

With Lizzie in good hands we flew home.

## 12

### TENNESSEE, ALABAMA, THE TOMBIGBEE RIVER

The weather was somewhat more endurable when we arrived back at Hales Bar Marina on the Tennessee river, September 26. Lizzie M looked great and Bob and Avis said that the last two months had been without incident. It was a few degrees cooler and the humidity was nearer normal.

After restocking with food and fuel we set off down the Tennessee to where we could branch off into the Tenn-Tom waterway. We anchored out as much as possible behind islands and in coves, some of which we had anchored in before. The weather stayed warm, and an occasional rain shower kept things clean and fresh. We swam often off the afterdeck in the warm clean fresh water. We spent our evenings watching the sunset while we enjoyed the evening's libation. The birds twittered and warbled, and the beautiful white herons and egrets searched the shallows for their evening meal. We watched the water go through its nightly change from blue, to silver, and sometimes gold, to black as the light faded. These were truly halcyon days.

Soon we were down at Pickwick Lake, the second lowest of the Tennessee lake system. Here, not far above the dam, we turned into a flooded area called Yellow Creek, and soon found a marina that had been recommended to us. We spent several days there getting some work done on the boat and restocking. Here at the small marina cafe I tasted my first Cajun cooking by ordering a bowl of Cajun chowder. It was delicious, I found out — after the numbing effect of the first bite had worn off.

Let me describe the route we were to travel. At the upper end of the Yellow Creek was a 30-mile canal. At the end of this was a swampy area of many creeks which ultimately combined to form the Tombigbee River. The Yellow Creek was a part of the Tennessee drainage which flowed down to the Mississippi and hence into the Gulf. This meant that there was a "continental" divide somewhere in that 30 miles of canal because the Tombigbee flowed down through Alabama to the Gulf of Mexico. The upper, shallow area was, of course, dredged and the water level was controlled by a series of low earthen dams.

Soon the Tombigbee grows large enough to be navigable in its own right, although there are still dams to help with flooding, and cover rapids. This upper area is called the Tenn-Tom waterway. About midway in the state, the

Black Warrior River adds its water to the Tombigbee and, just before Mobile, the Alabama River joins the Tombigbee. The Black Warrior is busy with commercial traffic all the way to Birmingham and the Alabama provides navigation to Montgomery.

The West knows little of this type of waterway system. Our western rivers are too violent to be navigable without giant dams. The Columbia is dammed to the Canadian border, but these giant structures were built primarily for power and have not generated near the commercial traffic envisioned by its advocates many years ago when the first dam at Bonneville was built. In addition, there has been a number of harmful effects. Many believe that these dams and the waterways that resulted were glorified much too heavily as to their benefits and belittled to heavily in the harm that has resulted. This author wishes to take no position and just enjoy the vast network that has resulted.

We must remember with a great deal of reverence the steam boats of Mark Twain's era who fought their way up these eastern rivers with cargos for the rich and fertile land of this great river system. With smoke-belching stacks and tooting whistles they carried cargos of manufactured goods to the farmers and returned bearing the bales and bushels of produce. They were vital to the building of this new and brawling country. Can you see them now? Handsome ladies with their wide hats and courtly gentlemen with their top hats and cigars, taking a turn around the ornate decks. Some, no doubt, spent the voyage in the gaming room, being fleeced by the riverboat gamblers.

Ah — 'twas a grand era, gone forever. But, as we sat on our afterdeck in the evening — hark! Was that the call of a cardinal or the toot of a whistle as the Alabama Belle rounds a bend? Was that the warble of a mocking bird or the strum of a banjo from the Betsy Lee as she passes on the other side of the island? That vanished time still lives in the hearts of romantics.

I have to say that upper Alabama state, as we saw it from the deck of our boat, is beautiful. Its rocky pine-studded islands reminded me of the San Juan Islands of the Pacific Northwest. As we proceeded south, we were just ahead of the fall colors. The gum trees and cypress were beginning to turn, but the willows, maples, and oaks were still in summer's green. Here we met again the tremendous live oaks that grow so huge as to make one wonder how they can sustain their own structure. We were told by the natives that the display of fall colors was so outstanding that steamboats from St. Louis and Nashville run excursions of several days up into this country and called them "Fall Color Tours."

Man himself sometimes outshines nature for fascination. In one of the river sections we passed a large flat barge secured to the town quay. On it were about 30 trailers and motor homes. Each was parked properly at an angle, and the owners had their awnings and lawn chairs out. A tug pushed the barge through the lakes and locks of the Tennessee River. If trailer travel and motor homes are your thing, here's a new idea.

We also got a great deal of amusement and pleasure out of being part of the life on the river. I almost felt like a latter day Mark Twain, had I not had difficulty with the language.

The Tombigbee had more commercial traffic and tug captains on it than any other place we had been. The

Mississippi may have had more tonnage but we seldom saw more than four or five tows in a day.

The tug captains have their own language, they nearly all talk in the drawling southern accent that is so pleasant to the ear, and so hard to understand at times. We soon became used to the phrases used, and by the time we reached the Gulf we could understand them quite well. For example, "See ya on one" was a phrase we heard often and used ourselves. Emily was pretty good at translating but at times even she was baffled by the sounds coming out of the radio speaker.

The VHF radio has replaced the whistle as a means of communication, but the traditions of the river are slow a-dying. Besides, "see yawn one" takes a lot less time to say than "Let us pass starboard to starboard," furthermore I don't think the salty talk of the sea ever was very prevalent on the freshwater highways of the continents.

It took us months to figure out this simple system. We first heard it when we heard one power boat telling another on the Intracostal Waterway, "I'll pass you on your one toot side." We referred to the Coast Guard regulations and could find nothing about "toots." We did find a regulation that said "One blast of the whistle means that you are changing course to the right. Two blasts — to the left." But did that relate to passing? It certainly did when you got into the Southern river systems. We learned quickly.

Soon we casually got on the radio and said something like, "Southbound sailboat to northbound tow, at mile 84, what's your pleasure, one or two?"

Back would come the reply, "Tug Betty Harper to southbound sailboat, see yawn one." (Translation — I will see you on the one whistle side.) He, then would ease to his right and we would ease to our right. It also works if you are overtaking another boat. You ask permission to pass on the "one whistle" side. The boat ahead needs to know this to avoid turning into you, or perhaps there is an obstruction ahead that would keep him from easing to his left.

Sometimes these exchanges would be followed by "Where ya'll from?" We've had several short but pleasant conversations with the captains. Most of them were quite business like, however. Once we rounded a gradual curve the tug ahead of us called us and said, "Tug Freedom to motor sailor, I'm going to need almost all the river to make the turn."

"If I move over to the bank will that be enough?" I replied.

"Yes, I think so, I just wanted you to know that I'll be cocked as I make that turn in order to head into the dock area on the other side."

"OK," I said, "I'll go clear over until I run out of water. By the way, how did you know we were a motor-sailor?"

"Hey, buddy, I'm a sailor at heart, I just drive this tug so that I can afford my sailboat."

The Tombigbee River winds like a tortured snake down to the Gulf and meanders in and out of the state of Mississippi. Each bend and major sandbar has a name. We quickly learned that the tug operators did not use mileposts that were clearly indicated on the charts. Tugs do not like to pass on sharp curves, nor do they like surprises. They talk to each other on the radio to the extent of their range — about 10 miles — and each plans their passings ahead. A typical exchange might go as follows:

"Tug Mary Belle approaching Whitehorse Bend,"

We heard a lot of this chatter as the tugs kept track of each other.

"Ah— h Tug Wildflower to Mary Belle. I'm here at about Stauffer dock, looks like we might meet in the curves there by Buzzard's Roost."

"Mary Belle to Wildflower, Yeah — whaddaya think?"

"Wildflower here, I've got a mile of straightaway coming up, I'll just nose into the bank and wait for you."

"Hate to ask you to do that, but it would cut down on the excitement."

"No problem, see ya soon."

Another point about river courtesy, it is important to not only announce our approach to a curve, but, also to mention that we were a pleasure boat. The reason for this is that we are the "burdened" boat since we are more maneuverable. The tows, depending on their size and weight, take hundreds of feet to turn and many hundreds of feet to stop. An incident will illustrate why.

As we approached a fairly sharp bend I picked up the mike and said, "This is the sailboat Elizabeth M approaching Bayou Rageet."

Immediately came a somewhat frantic call on the radio, "Did you say sailboat?"

"Yes, this is the sailboat Elizabeth M, a pleasure vessel."

"Oh, well, OK."

Just then the nose of a barge began to come around the bend. Not having heard clearly, he wasn't sure that I wasn't a tow, and if I was there was, no time to avoid a collision. As I said, tug pilots don't like surprises.

Late one afternoon as we approached Coffeyville

Dam, the lock keeper became quite friendly with us on the radio. Emily had called to tell him that we were about three miles away and that we planned to anchor in a small bay just above the dam. We know from experience both here and in Europe that the lockkeepers keep track of all the traffic on their waterway and we wanted to let him know that we would not be going down when we arrived at his dam. Some lockkeepers will hold their process when a boat is just a short distance away.

In a marvelous southern drawl, he recommended that we stop at Bob's Fish Camp dock, have a drink and then tie into a mess of the best fried catfish in the south. Then after we were full and rested we could go across the river and drop the hook in the old riverbed just across the new channel.

It sounded like a great idea were it not for two reasons. One: as we passed Bobs the dock didn't look big enough to moor anything larger than a 12 foot fishing boat. Secondly: fried catfish, especially when served with hush puppies, has a tendency to set heavily on the stomach.

The lockkeeper promised to contact us on the radio in the morning when the locks were ready for us. We were up and ready with a quick breakfast by 0700. 0800came. 0900came. A barge came out, another went in, another came out. Then our old friend tug Harry Brindell was told to go in. I at once called the lock, but got no reply.

Finally, "Elizabeth M, this is Coffeyville."

"This is Elizabeth M, go ahead."

"Will you and that power boat that is anchored in the bay come up close to the lock and stand by, as soon as Harry Brindell is in I want you two to come in behind Harry Brindell and tie up, you'll go down with him."

"Roger," I said, "We were wondering if you had forgotten us."

"Not a chance," he said, "Those first two barges were red flags and we are not allowed to let any other craft in the lock with them." Red flags are flown on barges carrying hazardous cargo.

I felt a little foolish for thinking bad thoughts about lock keepers. Harry Brindell had a couple of loads of coal and a couple of logs and a scruffy looking work barge and no red flags.

A "load" is, of course, a loaded barge, and the alternative is "I have two empties."

I do not know who Harry Brindell (the man) was, but there appears to be a rather common practice of naming tugs after former captains, so he may have been a tug captain. The other practice, better known, is to name the tug after a wife or sweet-heart. This introduces a practice common among boaters of all sizes and persuasions. We frequently do not recall the last names of other boaters. We refer to most of our cruising friends as Kellog and Diana of Swan or Don and Rhoda of Sunchaser. This mentality carries over into commercial vessels also. Therefore it was perfectly natural for us to refer to Harry Brindell as a "friend."

The reason we had thought of Harry Brindell as a friend is that earlier on the Tennessee we had been waiting for a couple of hours for the lock to clear of a barge that had to be broken up. That phase finished the lockkeeper had ordered Harry Brindell into the lock. On the radio "Harry" had asked the lockkeeper to let us come in behind him as he wasn't going to need much of the lock.

Now, we carefully nudged in behind him. We tied

to the empty bollard, and the power boat tied alongside Harry. We were soon down to the lower level and Harry inched out of the lock. As soon as he was clear, the power boat roared out and was gone. We moved out also and then revved up and passed Harry Brindel on the one-whistle side.

Twenty minutes later, we heard Harry talking to the lockkeeper. His barge was hung up on a sandbar, which had worried us when we had passed him. The lockkeeper said that he would "dump the pit" to help him off. This, we finally reasoned out, consisted of filling the lock chamber with water and then letting it rush out. This momentarily increased the depth of water where the barge was aground and added some current to it. He did this three times until we heard Harry say "OK, that got her! Do they plan to do anything about this bar?"

Lock keeper, "Yes, the dredge is on the way down here now, but they got 30 miles to go yet and they only make 1 mile per hour." Obviously no one water skis behind a dredge.

We saw Harry Brindell one more time. We had travelled many miles between white chalky cliffs, which had provided some spectacular scenery. We planned to stop at a new port that was indicated on the charts at the Mississippi town of Espy. There they had carved out of the white chalk cliffs a square harbor about 100 feet wide and 600 feet long. The sides were nearly vertical, and the harbor was not yet equipped with places to tie to, so we just dropped the anchor.

When we arrived the entrance was blocked by a cable helping to retain a small dredge that was working there. As we hesitated, wondering what to do next our radio crackled and a voice said, "Hi there sailboat, you want to go in?"

"Well, yes," Emily answered, "but it looks like the harbor is closed."

"No problem," said the voice, "We'll just drop the cable and you go right on in."

They did, and we did.

A little while later a rough work boat disconnected from the barge and came over to our boat. The man in the bow, a nice looking fellow, after going through the usual, "Are you really from Oregon?" routine, said that he had purchased the dredge in Oregon and shipped it across the country to the Tombigbee. He even knew how to pronounce Willamette and Oregon properly. For the uninitiated, Willamette is the name of one of two large rivers that flow through Portland and it is pronounced Wil-lam'-it, not Wil-ya-met'. Oregon is pronounced Or-e-gun, not Or-e-gone.

He offered to take us into town for shopping or, if we wanted, to get something for us. We needed nothing, but appreciated this kind gesture, so typical of the southerners. I, too, being a raging conservative, very much admired his entrepreneurship in creating this business for himself without any dependency on the government. These small businesses are the real strength of our America!

What has all this got to do with Harry Brindell? The next morning as we were preparing to get underway, a tug went by. Emily almost shouted, "There's Harry Brindell! See the two loads of logs and the two of coal? And look in the entrance, there's the work barge that he was pushing!"

"Yes"! I exclaimed excitedly, "and now he is going back upstream to unload his logs and coal." I don't know why we were so excited, but we had just seen an old friend on the river and we almost got on the radio to say hello. But, we really didn't know either of the captains, and we are a little shy. And we really weren't a part of the river life, just passing through, and besides they probably don't like pleasure boats cluttering up their river. I wish we had talked to them. Since they were southerners, I'm sure they would have been delighted to respond. But, for a moment there, we felt a kinship with these latter-day rivermen.

We moved down the river into alligator country. We searched the beaches and looked carefully up creeks and sloughs.

No success. We met a couple in a small power boat that stopped to chat one evening while we were anchored. They had been searching for alligators and were reporting their sightings to some office. They were not officials, but amateurs who enjoy wandering through the swamps and were helping with the alligator census at the same time. They had seen several.

We did, however, see a multitude of birds and a few other animals. Deer appeared occasionally and once we observed a cute pair of muskrats romping near their hole. Snow white egrets, herons and buzzards were plentiful. We saw one bald eagle and a few osprey. Mockingbirds sang in the trees when we were anchored. My favorite, the mockingbird, entertained us frequently with its incredible repertoire. They do "mock" other birds, and you will frequently hear the call of a robin or a meadowlark mixed in with three or four minutes of successive trills, warbles, whistles and chirps. The kingfishers amused us as they darted across our path scolding us for invading their realm. There are not many sights more beautiful than to see a snow white egret stalking majestically among the cyprus knees searching for his supper as the sun drops behind the trees. This was our evening's entertainment.

As we got closer to Mobile, industry began to make its appearance. Paper mills are a new and rapidly growing industry of the South. The two loads of logs that Harry Brindell was carrying were, undoubtedly destined for a chipper plant. These plants are frequently located along the river so that barges could transport the logs and then load up with chips to take to the paper mills.

We passed several chip yards and the machinery is tremendous. A giant crane picks up bundles of these "logs" and drops them into a hopper and chips are blown out of the other side. I put "logs" in quotes because the trees there in the south are harvested when they are only six to nine inches in diameter. In the Pacific Northwest we let them grow for 40 more years before harvesting. The trees here in the south, free from the spotted owl problem, are treated as a crop, and small trees make good chips, too.

I hope I have not bored you with this, but to me it is a fascinating industry. It does have one problem. As we passed one paper mill a large pipe was discharging a smelly brown liquor directly into the stream. The three or four foot wide trail curved down the river with the current and we traveled several miles before its stain disappeared. The odor resembled rotten eggs and stung our nostrils. In the Northwest, industry has cleaned up our rivers at their own, not inconsequential, expense. It is not easy for them to compete with mills here in the South that avoid this expense. I have been described as a feisty old curmudgeon, and Emily and I have spent most of our lives enjoying the outdoors. As a result we were angered by such blatant pollution.

We continued southward and were soon in the industrial areas of Mobile. Industry seems to concentrate on waterfronts and although it is great for the industry, it is depressing for the cruiser who has just emerged from some rather pristine wilderness. We hurried through Mobile and emerged into Mobile Bay.

About ten miles down the bay was the Dog River Marina. This was our destination, but getting there was not easy for several reasons. First: although Mobile Bay was a large bay it was quite shallow and Elizabeth M, with her deep draft, could get there only by following explicit instructions that we had received as far back as St. Louis. Secondly: it was approaching low tide as we entered the bay, and it would take us about two hours to go ten miles. We would be trying to find it at the least optimum time. To further compound the problem, we had phoned the marina and they had given us new directions somewhat different from past advice.

Sticking strictly to the ship channel, we proceeded out into the bay. Earlier directions had insisted that we must turn 90 degrees to the right at a certain marker and follow some markers into the entrance to Dog River. (A marker is a pole stuck into the bottom with either a red triangle, or a green square on it. They are all numbered and shown on the chart in their precise location. All green squares are on the left side when you come into port in the U. S. buoy system. The rest of the world places the green squares on the right).

We reached the marker where the right turn would have been made and could see the line of markers leading into Dog River. But the marina owner had said on the phone that with our draft we would be better off to go about

2 miles farther along the channel and then angle back toward the entrance to the river.

This we did but it cost us a lot more time. Without channel markers to guide us we moved quite slowly at about two knots. We felt our way with one eye on the depth sounder. Occasionally the clearance with the bottom was measured in inches. It was getting late in the day when we finally poked our bow into Dog River. The attractive, but small, bridge opened quickly for us. Just past it was the marina and we tied tiredly up to the outer pier and reported our presence to the marina. No one answered so we just cooked a light supper and went to bed without even going ashore.

We planned to stay there and refit. Refitting is another term for fixing everything that is wrong on the boat and adding those new things that you feel you need. One problem that we vowed to fix was the electrical system. It had been giving us trouble ever since Ft. Lauderdale. A second was to replace the radar which had been malfunctioning. In addition, we were now headed back to the ocean and would need a life raft and other survival gear. All this would take time and money. We had lots of the former, but no excess of the latter.

At this point in our life we had no firmly entrenched plans or schedule. There was only one imperative and that was to close the loop of our circumnavigation of the eastern U. S. by returning to Florida.

## 13

### CLOSING THE CIRCLE

We left Mobile, Alabama on 10 December, 1991. Our first stop was Pensacola, Florida, and up to that point our route was in "protected" waters. An Intracoastal Waterway does girdle the Gulf of Mexico and stretches from Southern Florida to Southern Texas. It is not as well maintained or marked as the ICW on the East Coast, and I think it was used during WWII to avoid the marauding German subs that were brazenly trying to make a German lake out of the Caribbean.

The Pensacola area, to us at least, seemed unduly blessed with white sand beaches. They scintillated and sparkled in the bright winter sunlight. The other great attraction at Pensacola was the Naval Air Museum. We were able to actually touch aircraft that filled us with pride when we were teenagers: Admiral Byrd's polar plane, to mention one, and many flying clipper ships.

We departed Pensacola at 0900, 16 December to sail directly to Tampa. This was an "overnighter", meaning that it would take us about forty-eight hours to make the crossing. That would translate into two nights at sea. It would be our first night at sea for nearly three years. At that time of year, the local knowledge said to wait until a weather front passed through and then to follow it south. Following this advice, we left and were blessed with a good breeze from the North which filled our sails beautifully — until about 1600 (4:00 P.M.). The wind died so we turned on the motor. All was calm and beautiful including the starry night. Our night watches turn out to be some of those moments that you cherish for a long time.

I awakened Emily at 0400 for her watch and turned into my bunk. She caught me just as I was drifting down-down-down into the heavy sleep of a happy man and said, "The auto-helm is acting funny."

A few tests and volatile expressions later, we decided that we were nearly out of electricity. Translation — the battery is dead! We had just spent quite a few dollars to improve our electrical system and had purchased two new batteries, which explained the volatility of our expressions. We decided to save what power we had left in the batteries for the loran and to hand-steer the rest of the way thus saving the electricity required by the automatic pilot. We also decided to navigate without lights at night but turn them on whenever we saw another vessel.

Another problem was that the compass light was not very bright and made reading the compass difficult in the dark. Ordinarily this presents no problem as we only use the compass to set the course for our auto-helm and leave the minute rudder adjustments up to the auto-helm. Now, we would have to hand steer for another thirty-six hours with eyes glued to the compass making those minute adjustments every minute by hand.

Our flashlight solved the light problem and we steered by various stars cutting down the time we needed to check the compass. During the day it was easier to steer by the compass but with no stars to steer by the concentration was more demanding. The horizon was featureless, although occasionally we could steer toward a prominent cloud, but most of the time we had to keep our eyes glued to the compass to keep from wandering off course.

Every two hours we turned on the loran to see if we were on course and made a dot on our chart. For thirty-six hours we stood half-hour watches and watched those dots creep toward our destination. We planned to enter the waterway just north of Tampa at Clearwater, one of the few dredged entrances to the waterway. Also it was the closest point of refuge that might have repair facilities. Drenched with fatigue, we arrived at the Clearwater sea buoy. With Emily backing me up we negotiated the entrance and by 1145 were tied up at the Clearwater Marina.

Our batteries charged during the night while hooked up to shore power so the next day we elected to go on into the Tampa City Marina. Our adventures were not quite over. To get to the marina we had to go out into the center of Tampa Bay and pass under a huge bridge. The wind had strengthened to a small gale, and, although we knew that it might be rough "out there" we decided to press on to the marina. Shortly after passing under the bridge we took several tons of water over the bow. After we had recovered, I noticed that we were only doing about two knots against the wind and waves. Dividing this into the ten miles we had to go gave us a question and the answer: "Five more hours of this? No way!"

We went back into the waterway and found a marina for the night, and then moved to another marina that was better equipped to handle storm conditions. We repaired the electrical problem, went home for the holidays and returned later to continue our adventures.

Our dreams had been realized. We had set out to do something and, in spite of our "senior" status had succeeded. We had explored the eastern U. S. via most of its waterways and returned to that most glamorous of American states, Florida. With this voyage we had so broadened our cruising life style that we wonder to this day if it was really all true. Yes, it was. It awaits those sailors and adventurers of all ages who care to challenge their horizons.

*Come my friends,*
*'Tis not too late to seek a newer world.*
*Push off, and sitting well in order smite*
*The sounding furrows. For my purpose holds*
*To sail beyond the sunset, and the baths*
*Of all the western stars, until I die.*

Tennyson's, Ulysses

# The History of the Erie Canal

Excerpted from **"Cruising Guide to the Erie Canal"**, by Tom Kranz; Rebecca Smith, editor. Published by, Longacres-North American Entertainment, Inc., 1529 Mill Road, East Aurora, NY 14052.

In 1808 the New York Assembly authorized the construction of a canal across New York State. Several different routes were surveyed, and a report was forwarded to President Thomas Jefferson in the hopes of securing federal funding for the project. Jefferson, however, felt that a canal of that magnitude — stretching across rivers, valleys, and mountains — was a century ahead of its time, and there the matter rested.

At the same time, the New York legislature created a canal commission to borrow money on the State's credit. Governor DeWitt Clinton promised his support, eventually becoming the driving force behind the movement which led to the authorization of the construction of the Erie Canal. The legislature passed the canal law on April 15, 1817.

Groundbreaking ceremonies were held on July 4, 1817, in Rome, New York, where digging began east to west.

The Erie Canal was 40 feet wide at ground level, 28 feet wide at the bottom, and only 4 feet deep.

The engineers and surveyors — most of whom had no knowledge of how to build a canal — invented a system of eighty-three locks to enable the canal to climb the 571 feet from the Hudson River to Lake Erie.

Eighteen aqueducts were built to carry the canal over deep ravines and white water rivers. The Genesee Aqueduct, 808 feet long, was the longest stone arch bridge in North America. But because it leaked, it was replaced twenty years later by a longer and wider aqueduct, which still exists. On Octover 26, 1825, Governor Clinton steppped on board the SENECA CHIEF in Buffalo, officially opening the Erie Canal. He proclaimed it the "Eighth Wonder of the World." Cannons placed at ten mile intervals along the entire length of the Erie Canal and down the Hudson River to New York City thundered!

The first cruise along the Erie Canal began: it took the SENECA CHIEF and her passengers ten days to reach New York Harbor, and when the Governor poured Lake Erie water into the water in the harbor, the "Marriage of the Waters" ceremony turned into the biggest parade and ball in the history of New York City. Thomas Jefferson, John Adams, James Madison, James Monroe, John Quincy Adams, Andrew Jackson — all who originally laughed at the prospect of the waterway — and many other dignitaries of the day, were in attendance for the ceremonies.

The importance of the Erie Canal to the early economic development of New York State, and the expansion of the United States, can hardly be overemphasized. By providing an all-water outlet from the Great Lakes to New York Harbor, the canal shortened travel time between Buffalo and New York City from six weeks to ten days. As a result, New York City quickly overtook Philadelphia and Boston in becoming the major seaport city in the country. Buffalo, which was a wilderness outpost of 200 in 1812, became a bustling city of 18,000 by 1840, and the major trade center of the West.

Corn, wheat,oats, hides, and lumber from the western United States came through Buffalo via the Great Lakes, and traveled eastward to Albany and south to New York City along the canal. Manufactured goods brought into New York Harbor traveled westward, and this commerce led to the tremendous expansion of the interior of the United States.

The canal also stimulated the growth of sleepy New York towns such as Albany, Utica, Syracuse, and Rochester. New cities — Lockport, Brockport, Spencerport, Fairport, and Middleport — were born as the workers decided to live on the canal. The veritable explosion of commerce along the canal eventually gained New York the title of"The Empire State."

The Erie Canal proved extremely successful, and it paid handsome profits in spite of the great cost of construction. Betweeen 1836 and 1862, the canal was deepened to seven feet. This enabled larger canal boats carrying 240 tons of cargo, rather than the standard 30 tons, to use the canal.

However, construction and revenues suffered from a financial panic, and from the beginnings of competition from the railroads. By 1898, it became apparent that if the Erie Canal was to survive into the 20th Century, major enlargements would not be enough.

At New York State Governor Theodore Roosevelt's urging, New Yorkers approved what was, in 1901, the largest single bond issue any state had ever provided — $101 million to dramatically change the present canal. Construction of the Barge Canal began in 1903 and was completed in 1918. The new canal ran parallel to the original Erie, canalizing existing rivers and streams to a depth of 12 feet. Fifty-seven locks were built — 300 feet long and 43.5 feet wide — accommodating barges carrying up to 3,000 tons of cargo, with lifts of six to forty feet. The lock design was updated and the locks were now operating electronically, opening and closing within thirty seconds.

## THE CANAL TODAY

The Barge Canal of the early 1900's has become the New York State Canal System of today. The Erie, Champlain, Oswego, and Cayuga and Seneca Canals make up one of the world's greatest inland waterway systems. These canals provide a renewable source of clean energy for the residents of New York State. The hydro power sites along the system provide the State with over $100 million worth of power every year.

The New York State Canal System is used to monitor the water storage capacity of the many waterbodies throughout New York State. Farmers use the system for irrigation, and many communities rely on the canals for their fresh water supply.

Although the original flavor of the Erie Canal is no longer present in the New York State Canal System, the continuing benefits are obvious to the residents of New York State and to those who cruise the system. The New York State Canal System — rich with history — is a living tribute to the men who built the original Erie Canal.